x D Duddy

Best Wishes
to Greg.
1989 -
10 - 24.

Visual Aesthetics

J J de Lucio-Meyer

visual aesthetics

Icon Editions
Harper & Row, Publishers
New York, Evanston, San Francisco, London

FIRST U.K. EDITION 1973
PUBLISHED BY LUND HUMPHRIES, LONDON

FIRST U.S. EDITION 1974

ISBN : 0–06–435665–5 (cloth)
        0–06–430052–8 (paper)

LIBRARY OF CONGRESS CATALOG CARD NUMBER : 74-120

Frontispiece :
The linear character of
our time
caught by the camera of the
author

Corrigendum
page 192 Caption to read :
James Whistler
(1834–1903)
The fiddler
etching with dry-point
10×7½ in
Victoria and Albert Museum, London

Designed by J. J. de Lucio-Meyer
Made and printed in Great Britain by
Lund Humphries, Bradford and London

to my friends near and far

Introduction

This book is intended for an educated and enquiring public who realize that art and design are becoming increasingly important in everyday life but who need a short and comprehensive introduction to the subject. It is hoped that the book will inspire the reader to observe more acutely and critically his environment in order that he might take an active part in improving it.

Visual aesthetics is an attempt to bridge the gap between the orthodox method of teaching art appreciation, which is mainly historical, and the modern approach to design theory which is predominantly visual.

It is an essentially down to earth, non-mystical approach which links up movements in the visual arts with related fields such as the theatre and music. However, it does deal with psychological and philosophical concepts, but in simple terms.

The illustrations are not supplementary but are a necessary and integral part of the book and reveal both the analysis and the subsequent development of the principles.

The book presents a logical analysis of art and design movements in order to establish the principles which lie behind them. It begins with the components and shows how these are applied in the style and expression of art and design.

There are two parts to the book. Each part contains four chapters. The first part is principally concerned with the fundamentals of art and their application or use by the artist and designer.

The chapter *Line and Expression* describes the linear character of our time and the visual dialogue created by lines in art, design and architecture. Besides visual theories, the final part of this chapter gives a complete account of the aesthetic approach through the ages up to contemporary expression.

In *Area, Space: Composition* the chapter begins with a consideration of area and space in painting, sculpture, architecture and design. It goes on to deal with the idea of the golden section at different periods and concludes with a look at modules and their application in the modern world.

Creative Light and Colour is concerned with light and movement in art, the theatre and cinema as well as giving a thorough account of colour personality, and the symbolic use of colour in different civilizations and societies. It suggests experimental work and refers to modern colour engineering and the principal theories held about colour at different times.

Under the heading *Structure, Surface, Texture* an examination is made of the possibilities and limitations of different materials and an analytical account is given of structure and its characteristics, including speed and optical illusion. A description of related structure and the structural aspects of functional design forms part of this chapter.

The second part of the book deals largely with the philosophic and aesthetic aspects of art and design.

The chapter *Vision and Rhythm* is an introduction to the whole subject of creativity. It begins with a brief study of the human senses and goes on to the artist's vision, the public's perception and the aesthetic sensation. In this way the reader is led on from the simple to the more difficult. Articulate and inarticulate form and the creation of rhythm and of points of visual interest are also to be found in this account.

In *Looking at Art* an evaluation is made of the employment of form and shape and some experiments of the modern movement are analysed. It is concerned with distortion and comprehension in art, and the complex subject of movement and motion as expressed by different artists. It represents the present time as the dynamic age with its Kinetic art, Op, Pop and Television and Film. The idea of tension in art is also examined.

Criticism and Philosophy is the heading of a chapter dealing with the phenomena of art and design, and containing a comparison of aesthetic and surrealistic aspects and some references to established and experimental theories. It searches for an explanation of and a dialogue with the work of art, and reviews its content, physique and function and its very *raison d'être,* involving the changing outlook from pre-eighteenth-century patronage to the new artistic freedom in Eastern and Western societies.

Finally, the chapter on *Art, Design and Style* draws together ideas on the value of historical experience and puts forward some suggestions for the guidance of the reader in further study. It poses the question whether the history of art should be an analysis or recording and considers the direction of art and design today and its implications for tomorrow.

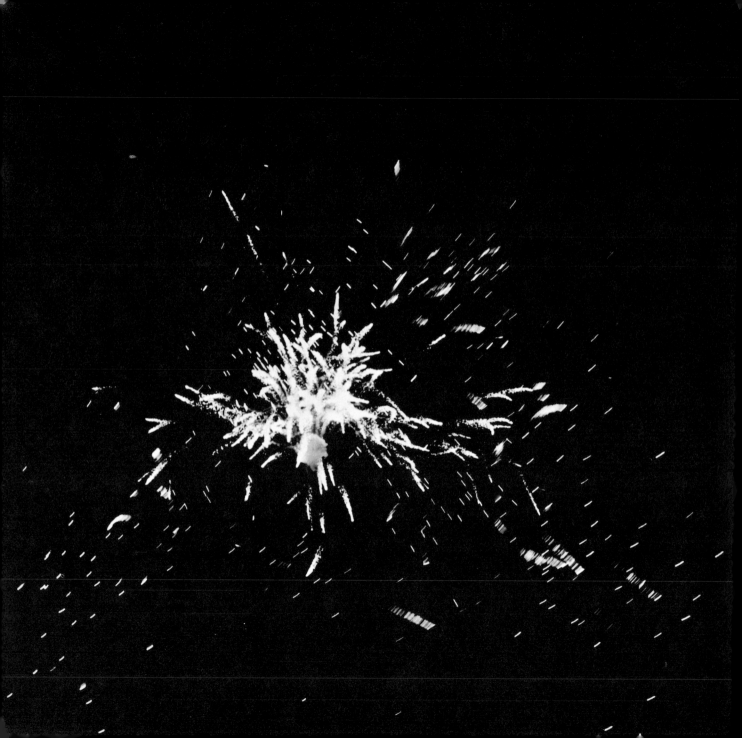

Line and expression

Line and expression
created by fireworks on the
Côte d'Azur
photographed by the author

This aerial view reveals the lines
of modern beauty, although
entirely based on function :
a high-speed motorway
leading to the south

1968 Claes Oldenburg
Soft scissors
canvas filled with kapok
painted with liquitex,
7 pieces, ranging from
24 to 72 inches long,
72 × 35 × 6 inches over-all
Pasadena Art Museum

The line of beauty

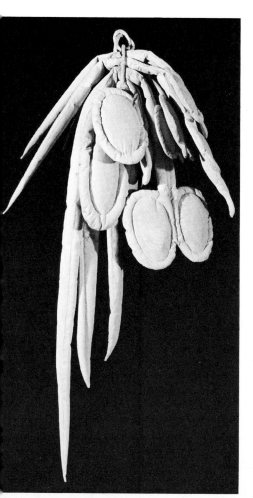

'It is to be observed, that *straight lines* vary only in length, and therefore are least ornamental. That *curv'd lines* as they can be varied in their degrees of curvature as well as in their length, begin on that account to be ornamental. That straight and curv'd lines joined, being a *compound line,* vary more than curves alone, and so become somewhat more ornamental. That the *waving line*, or line of beauty, varying still more, being composed of two curves contrasted, becomes still more ornamental and pleasing . . . and that the *serpentine line*, or line of grace, by its waving and winding at the same time different ways, leads the eye in a pleasing manner along the continuity of its variety.'

This was written by William Hogarth in the *Analysis of Beauty*, published in London in 1753. It reads almost like a modern instruction book although written some 200 years ago. In fact it could not have been written today. In Hogarth's time the line was considered only as a supporting element for an ambitious figurative composition while in some modern art, especially non-figurative art, it has become a design element in its own right. This does not deprive Hogarth's argument of any of its merit because each period finds its own way of artistic expression and indeed analysis of beauty. The theory of the past can well serve for guidance, even though the artist of today is not concerned to adopt the attitudes of the old masters.

1967 Ben Nicholson
Half mug, half jug
etching
15×12¾ in (38×32·5 cm)
Marlborough Fine Art
London

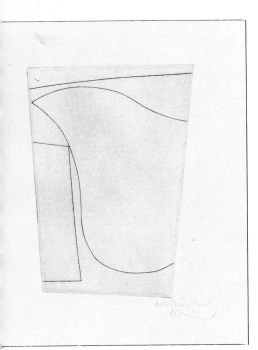

While ornamentation as such has to a great extent disappeared, the line occupies a crucial role in today's art, architecture and industrial design, in fact in our whole environment. Simple observation of things we see every day can help to reveal the linear character of our time, for example, neon-lights on advertising hoardings. The line on its own is often applied in design and can replace verbal communication, e.g. at the entrance to theatres and cinemas. Often the eye of the spectator is led into such entrances by a diminishing and receding series of lines.

The banal question 'What's your line?' is, nevertheless, revealing because the *line*, in our time, is very often considered identical with *characteristic.* Expressions such as line of fashion, stream-line, line of production all express the speed of change for which our age is known. The dynamic character of our time involves travelling, bridging distance. It is symbolized by the line, because geometrically the line is the shortest distance between two points. The line is the artery of modern life.

Philip Thompson
Cover design
geometrically the line is the
shortest distance between
two points, bridging distance

1965 Winfred Gaul
3 little roses
150×110 cm
Collection Dr Weinsziehr
Düsseldorf

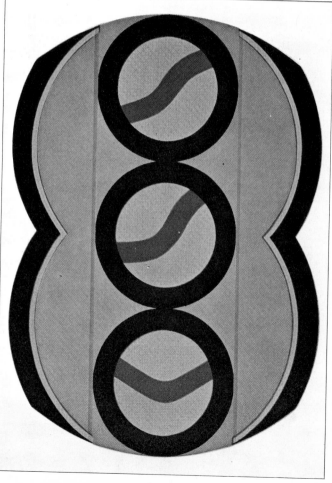

1963 Victor Pasmore
Black abstract
oil on board
60 × 60 in
Tate Gallery
London

The line, its force and speed

The line can create a visual relationship and is the most important means of communication between elements in the visual arts. A simple drawn line on its own which does not seem to have contact with the background and appears to stand upon it, can become part of it by combining with other lines. Two lines, placed opposite each other, create a visual dialogue or a visual communication. It is as though two people were confronting each other and conversing. The endless variations that can be achieved by placing two lines on a given area in different positions and by varying the height, volume, character, colour and texture of these two lines are described in the chapters on volume, rhythm, and composition. The line is the basis for any rhythmical grouping. For example, two lines on one side and three lines on the other side of a given area will create not only a dialogue, but also an interesting grouping — which could be compared to two groups of people talking to each other. Before, however, analysing in more detail the rhythmical possibilities and optical illusions that can be created by lines, let us look at the line on its own.

While on its own, the line can divide the area on which it is placed, to create either harmony or dynamic tension. There certainly is a difference in the aesthetic sensation resulting from a line placed exactly in the centre of an area, whether this is vertical or horizontal, and an asymmetrical arrangement. Attaching the line to one side of the area only, will give it movement, force and speed. The same can be achieved by adding another form element, such as a point, to a symmetrically arranged line. But in a symmetrical position, the line

1969 Marcello Morandini
Design no 53
61 × 82 cm
private collection

1968–69 Marcello Morandini
Sculptures
private collection

1936 Karl Schmidt-Rottluff
Spiegelnder See
oil on canvas
76·7 × 112·2 cm
Museum Folkwang
Essen

1970 Victor Pasmore
Linear development 3
screenprint
18½ × 18½ in (47 × 47 cm)
Marlborough Fine Art
London

Carel Visser
Woodcut I
on Japanese paper
21·5 × 80 cm
Centraal Museum
Utrecht

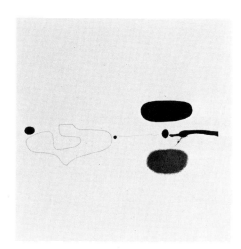

shows no more than its own character — being static and immobile and full of classical dignity. An additional form element will make it 'travel', so to speak. Furthermore, two points placed opposite each other will create a kind of imaginary line because the eye naturally desires to bridge the uncomfortable gap and continues 'travelling' between these two points, a kind of 'wishful seeing'. This experience is akin to that of a person looking for the two points on a map between which he intends to travel. Here, the eye will perform exactly the same 'bridging-the-gap' activity, which is based on the human tendency to 'wishful thinking'. A line in the centre, contrasted by one element such as a square or a circle, will make the composition appear off-balance, thus creating tension and attracting attention. The balance will be redressed by reducing the weight of the other element, for example, by employing a paler or lighter shade of colour for the element or by dissolving it into a tint of fine lines or a pattern of a passive and harmonious nature. By this last procedure, however, the line itself will be strengthened.

1968 Winfred Gaul
Swinging orange
114×147 cm
private collection

1970 Michael Bolus
1st sculpture
68½×132×84 in
McAlpine Gift
Tate Gallery
London

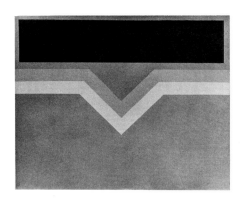 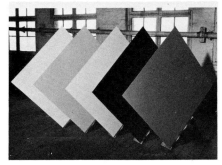

The diagonal line is often employed by those searching for visual excitement and sensation. Most elements of architecture and landscape are based on verticals and horizontals and even the basic activity of ordinary human movement is essentially horizontal and vertical, but the diagonal in art gives just as much optical sensation as a non-visual activity which is diagonal, such as mountain-climbing, travelling up or down a hill, or the crescendos and diminuendos in music. This diagonal movement can also be compared with the jumps of a dancer or the pacing of a person walking, because by lifting the leg, a diagonal activity, movement is created. Diagonal movement is often closely related to rotating movement, which is the basis of all movement; but diagonal movement and rhythm are certainly more forceful, and, as a design element, the diagonal line is more forceful than the circle.

1927 Wassily Kandinsky
Drawing
pen and ink
19×12⅝ in (48·3×32 cm)
Marlborough Fine Art
London

1965 Shigeo Fukuda
Romeo and Juliet
a modern approach with
abstract linear illustrations
published in Tokyo ;
author's collection

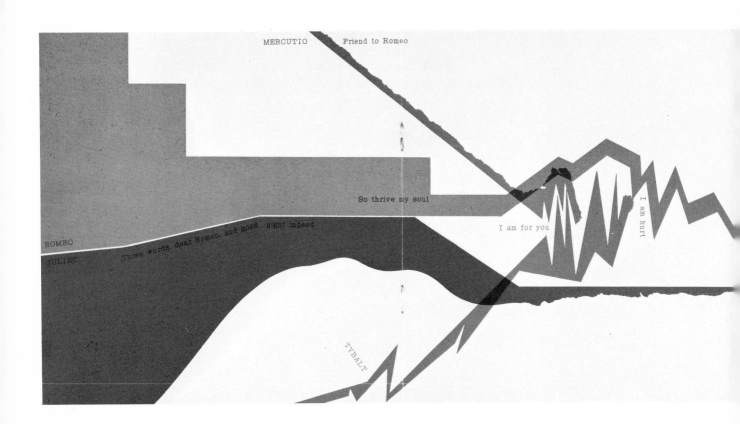

1970 Robert Motherwell
Africa 5
screenprint
31¾ × 23⅝ in
Marlborough Fine Art
London

Interrupted, as shown in the composition on the left, the diagonal line will be more forceful than a vertical or horizontal one : it will attract the attention and not just bridge the gap ; it will create a feeling of 'being left in the air' or of two forcefully opposing elements which, for example, in a poster for the prevention of accidents could well symbolize two cars crashing. Psychologically, it would appear that a diagonal running from the left-hand bottom corner to the right-hand top has an *ascending* quality, expressing optimism, and *joie de vivre* – while a diagonal from the left-hand top to the right-hand bottom corner would appear to have a *descending* quality and is often interpreted as pessimistic, forecasting danger, accidents, falling, misery and experiences one would rather avoid in life. It is interesting to observe that the ascending diagonal often has the climbing quality of a vertical, though it is more pronounced, and in addition it can sometimes almost acquire the tranquil character of a horizontal, though it is just a little more cheerful and fascinating.

But these observations cannot be generalized since they depend on the perception and reaction of the observer and on the exact 'body' of the volume, on the colour, on the textural quality and, most important, on the composition as a whole. Combining a horizontal or descending diagonal with a pure vertical, will certainly reduce the 'falling' effect, as shown in the next illustration, and will be registered by the eye as an element of introduction to the ascending vertical. Almost the same can be said about the free composition of a greater number of lines. Such a 'wild' composition of lines may express chaos and collapse but, cleverly

1969 Barbara Hepworth
Winter Solstice
from portfolio of 12 screenprints
'opposing forms'
31 × 23 in (78·7 × 58·5 cm)
Marlborough Fine Art
London

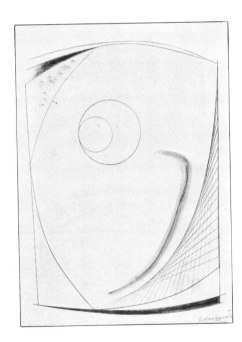

arranged, they could express the exact opposite, sound structure and order. While a straight line has an unchangeable direction and is visually quite plain, a distortion or a change of direction of the line gives visual excitement. These special effects are sought by the photographer who tilts his camera and in doing so he acts in a similar way to the painters of the Expressionist, Cubist and Fauve movements, who all distorted the lines of faces, figures, towns and landscapes for emotional emphasis.

Curved lines can express dynamism and movement: for instance, waves of the sea, moving clouds, the majestic contours of steep mountains; the growing form of flowers, plants, leaves and branches of trees; a moving animal of any kind, a horse, a tiger; and streamlined forms of transport such as aeroplanes. The line can not only suggest volume, shape and form, but can also embrace space. This can be demonstrated by a curved line: a semicircle into the inner shape of which, for instance, a vertical or horizontal is placed, or a horse-shoe shape into the open side of which a vertical or horizontal is inserted. An interesting optical observation: although it is usually much smaller in size and weight, the object or design element inside will be perceived by the eye first, while the surrounding *larger* shape will be perceived only later.

1965 Peter Branfield
Poster
Council of Industrial Design
London

1956 Barbara Hepworth
Curved form
sculpture
35½ × 23½ × 26½ in
Tate Gallery
London

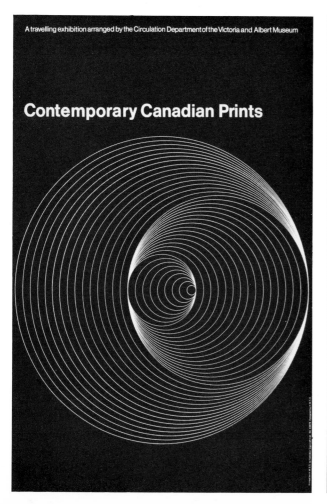

The direct contact

'Oh, that's a beautiful line' is often the first reaction of the public to the work of an artist or designer. Admiration for the personal 'handwriting' of an artist could not be better expressed. The line is often taken as being identical with the style and form of a particular person. The line is unambiguous, personal, honest. It is the direct and most intimate contact between the artist, his ideas and his inspiration, between the first sketch and the finally executed work of art or design – without interference or influence from an art movement or a fashion or from a compromise with a client : it is the artist's very own.

The line is also the first form element a child will use even before being able to produce any 'figurative' work. Mainly by wanting to imitate adults, but perhaps also through intuition, children seem to feel the line as the quickest and most immediate means of putting down ideas. In principle this is not much different from the grown-up artist and designer who captures his idea quickly on paper lest he might forget it. A child also naturally feels a circle, created by a linear scribble, as the best means of expressing and embracing volume, a whole ; applying it, without hesitation, equally to a human figure or a building.

The line reveals the visual training of the artist and designer and his knowledge of theory, i.e. the art he has studied. Most observers of art search, first of all, for the subject matter, e.g. man, house, landscape ; in other words they look at what the line represents. But it is revealing to look at the line itself from an aesthetic point of view, as the most

1837 Charles Darwin
*First notebook on transmutation
of species*
The linear expression
of a scientist's thought –
Darwin's theory of evolution

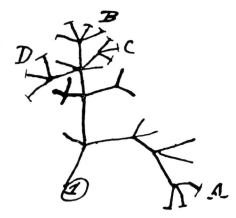

essential part of a composition in which movement, volume, shadow and texture are all represented and created by the line. The line can suggest anything : a shape or form by contour and outline ; a variety of types of composition by crossing, juxtaposition and overlapping. The line can indicate movement. It can also express volume. By contrast, in some art there is no sharp outline, but only 'built up' lines which suggest it.

Finally, a very simple observation : the line depends on the pressure on the paper by the artist. Very often an artist draws a line without thinking or planning and thus makes the line the true and spontaneous expression of himself. The non-rational aspects involved in analysing the emotional character which a line can have cannot be discussed in detail. Generations of artists and art critics have talked and written about these aspects, describing them as *the mystery of the line*. It can certainly be asserted that the line is responsible for certain aspects of the mystery of art ; these cannot be fully explained because a true dialogue between the creator of art and design and the observer comes about only by an act of the imagination.

1955 Hans Hartung
Composition T 55 – 18
oil on canvas
162·5 × 110 cm
Museum Folkwang
Essen

1970 Barbara Hepworth
Forms in a flurry
from portfolio of
12 screenprints 'opposing forms'
31 × 23 in (78·7 × 58·5 cm)
Marlborough Graphics
London

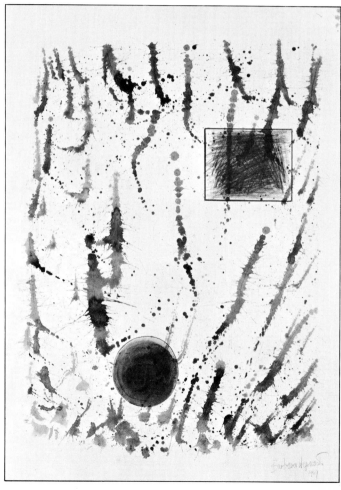

A means of expression

Studying the 'history' of the line can serve to show the ever-changing attitude towards form in art and design. Cave drawing, the first art of humanity in the Palaeolithic period (to about 10000 B.C.), has the outline as its beginnings, later to be filled in by simple linear texture and colour. Already in primitive times new materials led to the development of new forms, as is shown for example in a comparison of the shapes of an axe as the material changed from stone to metal (the stages to about 1000 B.C.) Different functional form also brought about a different style of line in the drawings of these eras. For Stonehenge, elongated stone blocks were selected that almost demonstrate perfect linear parallelism. Egyptian art (from about 4000 B.C.) is undoubtedly linear and the stylistic treatment of art is flat in painting and bas-relief and even in the surface treatment of sculpture and architecture. There is only restrained plastic *profondeur.*

The pyramid has flat linear surfaces and the obelisk, in its exterior form the very symbolism of linear art, is covered with hieroglyphics of equally linear nature. Greek art developed the flat forms of the Geometric stage (c.1100–400 B.C.), into the forms of the Hellenistic stage with lines now expressing volume and movement; this is especially so in the proportions of sculpture, a visual attitude that was basically adopted and modified by the Romans who introduced great richness of form.

In contrast, Early Christian art (from about A.D.200 to A.D.700), although at first borrowing form direct from Late Classical art, later developed a more linear form which was partly inspired by the flatness of bas-relief designs in the catacombs. The mosaics of Santa Maria Maggiore at Rome of the fifth century and of Sant'Apollinare in Classe and San Vitale at Ravenna of the sixth century may serve as examples. Architectural form was at first equally simple and linear in Early Christian art. When the Empire's capital was moved to Constantinople, in art, voluminous form again gave way to linear expression of comparative flatness. Under Byzantine rule the generously round form of Late Roman art became flat. The previously lively face became immobile. During this time, of course, the Western regions of the Empire were overrun by the Barbarians and later the Mediterranean region was occupied by the Arabs from Syria to Spain. After the dark ages, Carolingian and Romanesque art 'sorted out', so to speak, the cultural remains of the numerous invasions. Little architecture was left but there were illuminated manuscripts, created

2nd century B.C.
Aphrodite
Greek sculpture
bronze
height 38 cm
British Museum
London

A.D. 6th century
Notables of the court of Justinian
San Vitale
Ravenna

A.D. 698
Lindisfarne Gospels
full page illustration,
gospel of St Mark
British Museum
London

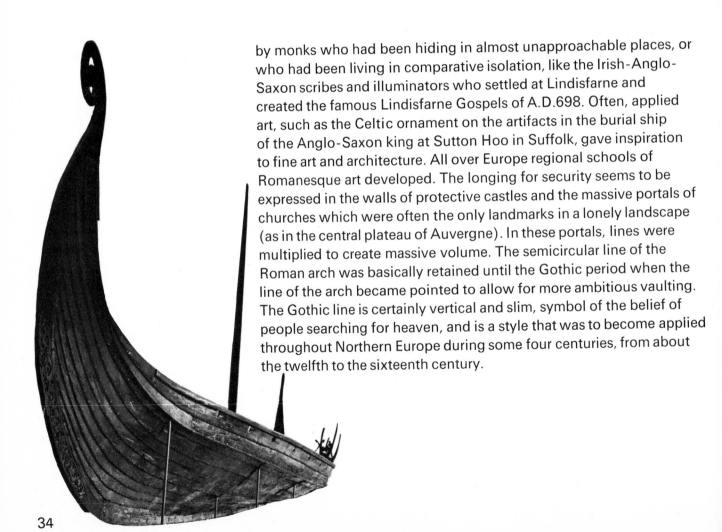

by monks who had been hiding in almost unapproachable places, or who had been living in comparative isolation, like the Irish-Anglo-Saxon scribes and illuminators who settled at Lindisfarne and created the famous Lindisfarne Gospels of A.D.698. Often, applied art, such as the Celtic ornament on the artifacts in the burial ship of the Anglo-Saxon king at Sutton Hoo in Suffolk, gave inspiration to fine art and architecture. All over Europe regional schools of Romanesque art developed. The longing for security seems to be expressed in the walls of protective castles and the massive portals of churches which were often the only landmarks in a lonely landscape (as in the central plateau of Auvergne). In these portals, lines were multiplied to create massive volume. The semicircular line of the Roman arch was basically retained until the Gothic period when the line of the arch became pointed to allow for more ambitious vaulting. The Gothic line is certainly vertical and slim, symbol of the belief of people searching for heaven, and is a style that was to become applied throughout Northern Europe during some four centuries, from about the twelfth to the sixteenth century.

11th century
*The multiplication of
the loaves and fishes*
capital
Saint Nectaire

12th century
Columnar statues
Chartres

Andrea del Verrocchio
(1436–88)
Young lady with a primrose
Bargello
Florence

1497–98 Albrecht Dürer
Babylon
woodcut
detail 15½ × 11¼ in
London Arts Gallery

Renaissance art turned its back on angular vertical Gothic art, which had never been widely popular in Italy, and went back directly to the art and architecture of the Romans which was now enthusiastically excavated and analysed by the artists of the period. The Renaissance also developed the painterly style which was to be followed by generations of artists. In this style the line is often neither contour nor a representation of volume. The line is only suggested, with a juxtaposition of masses acting as substitute. Leonardo was sometimes inspired by lines and spots to start a composition. The line of Dürer, especially in his woodcuts, gradually departing from Gothic simplicity, became, in its most refined technique, an element of Renaissance art. If analysed, Dürer's woodcuts show a combination of plain and dynamic lines which result in a brilliant expression of the eternal contrast of logic and temperament. The line of Michelangelo leads from the Renaissance and Mannerism to the beginning of Baroque art when volume and brightness and a manifoldly varied, vivid, curved line were the key note. While in Mannerism the line became a strict discipline, sometimes almost pedantically applied, and a tendency towards the vertical reappeared, Baroque art and architecture searched for a voluminous interplay of forms that was often based on the exploration of the horizontal. The creation of the English garden comes at the beginning of the eighteenth century when, for the first time, the landscape was no longer thought of as something to be crossed in order to arrive at a destination, as fraught with danger and with the possibility of accident, but as something beautiful to look at and to explore in pleasant promenade and fête.

Henri de Toulouse-Lautrec
(1864–1901)
Girl in the studio
gouache on cardboard
75×50 cm
Kunsthalle
Bremen

Auguste Rodin
(1840–1917)
Drawing
a sketch which has a fascinating
and very personal quality

This was the period of Rococo, which produced a line that was playful and light-hearted. A comparison of Boucher with his contemporaries Hogarth and Robert Adam demonstrates clearly the transition from Rococo *Spielerei* to a stricter neo-Classical line in the mid-eighteenth century.

Some 150 years of ever-changing modes, revivals, historicism and eclecticism were to follow, until just before the turn of the nineteenth century. Then Art Nouveau tried to create a new form of expression in art and design. Historical styles were forsaken in favour of the plant element, and a new language of line was found. In his poster art Toulouse-Lautrec found a linear style that was direct and *plakativ*. Van Gogh explored the expressive qualities of the line which made him in one sense a forerunner of the Expressionist movement. Some pioneers of modern art such as Matisse, Braque, Picasso, Léger, Mondrian and Rouault, although by no means restricted to experiments with line, have certainly based their activities on the properties of the line and this led them on to discover other aspects such as area, composition or colour. Fauvism and Cubism divide the composition by the line. Quite different in temperament, Constructivism and de Stijl search for a more rational, logical, purer approach. Klee, fascinated by the theory, makes a most valuable contribution to the discovery of the line in his creative work and his essays. This discovery has really only just begun. Every day, artists and designers are finding new modes of linear expression.

Emilio Brugalla Turmo
Discourses of Picasso
binding
Real Academia de Ciencias y Artes
Barcelona ;
a bookbinder's masterly
transformation of Picasso's images
into a linear abstract

1930 Paul Klee
Lines without end K 10
etching
7 × 5¼ in (17·8 × 13·4 cm)
Marlborough Fine Art
London

42

Area, space: composition

1953 Henri Matisse
Ivy in flower
collage
112×112 in
Albert and Mary Lasker Foundation,
Dallas Museum of Fine Arts

*c.*1890 Paul Cézanne
Man smoking a pipe
oil on canvas
92·5×73·5 cm
Kunsthalle
Mannheim

1909–10 Georges Braque
Mandola
28½ × 23½ in
Tate Gallery
London

The discovery of the area

While the line is mainly intellectual in character, the two-dimensional area is emotional, full of fantasy and activity. Enclosed by the line, the area provides the space within which the artist or designer can create ideas, just as in the geographical sense an area is a space within which one can live, play, work. The landscape viewed from an aeroplane is seen to be an essential part of the structure of living ; nature supplies a beautiful texture, an ensemble of vividly coloured areas. Modern art has, to no small extent, helped us to look at the area from a new point of view : as a form element in its own right. Air transport and mountain climbing have, in their turn, helped us to find a new perspective which man had dreamt of for centuries : the ability to fly, to look at the world from a majestic point of view, a bird's-eye view. When artists of the modern movement 'discovered' the area, they were fully aware that it had been used by artists of the past ; mainly during those periods before the Renaissance, before perspective was invented and the onlooker was led, so to speak, into 'perspective space' by the artist. The artists of the modern school attempted a new approach. This did not represent a return to medieval or Byzantine or early Egyptian or primitive art, art in which the artist told his story within the area provided and tried a kind of simple geometry to produce a feeling of space, i.e. to give a simple optical illusion of depth. Instead, the new approach attempted to treat problems of movement and colour in their own right, the area 'giving' them space to develop. Modern art searched for a more direct language without the detour resulting from the imitation of space and depth via geometrical perspective. Already in the Arts and Crafts movement

1913 Francis Picabia
Edtaonisl
oil on canvas
118¼ × 118⅜ in
Art Institute
Chicago

Picabia also claims to have painted the first abstract watercolour in 1908/09 which would antedate Kandinsky

and in Art Nouveau some artists and designers had declared passionately in favour of flat patterns for *objets d'art* and things for practical use such as carpets and wallpapers. Into this period, at the turn of the nineteenth century, falls the full development of poster art and Post-impressionist techniques which were sometimes inspired by oriental art. The future Cubists, studying the Cézanne memorial exhibition in Paris in 1906, became aware of the 'cube' — another term for the area. As early as 1905 the Fauves, with their spiritual leader Matisse, started with what they called the true element of art : the area. When in 1908 Matisse was criticized because his paintings only showed rough colouring of areas as practised in poster design, he defended his theory by stating that for him painting meant figurative representation developing out of the area. For him the area had an intrinsic worth, a *valeur*, it was an element which could interpret ideas as pure values of colour and line. The conception of space was now entirely spiritual, *l'espace spirituelle*, created entirely by the spiritual equivalent of area values in colour. Fauvism examined each element of structure singly : line, colour, volume, composition, and saw in art a synthesis of these, combined in the crucible of the artist's imagination. Fauvism respected fully not only the purity of materials but also the elements of space and good proportions, and saw them all as having an important part to play in creating art. When Kandinsky painted his first abstract watercolour in 1910, this was almost certainly the result of a long period of thinking in terms of the area. Others thought likewise, e.g. Vlaminck, Rouault, Nolde, Kirchner.

1912 Emil Nolde
Prophet
woodcut
12¾ × 8⅝ in (32·4 × 22 cm)
Marlborough Fine Art
London

The new concept of space

While Van Gogh had been searching for space, Mondrian, by contrast, had gradually tried to abstract space into compositions with less volume and more line. A comparison of Picasso and Mondrian in about 1910–11 reveals that both sometimes compose within an oval area, but Mondrian is more 'constructive' than Picasso, giving more architectural quality contrasted by tone values. The same conclusion can be reached by comparing Braque and Mondrian, as Braque was working closely with Picasso at this period on the principles of Cubism.

In this space age, an era when space is the key phrase not only in the vocabulary of the artist and designer but also in that of the technician, it is no surprise to find a growing appreciation among the public of the concept of space in art – a concept that was in fact developed long ago. The space concept in modern art has stirred the mind of the art lover and the art critic. It is not without interest that the 'discovery' of the term space by August Schmarsow in the late nineteenth century has, even in recent publications, been called 'troublesome' – to put it mildly. But the artist's conception of space, perhaps more than any other conception, may help to close the gap between art and public. The whole of modern life is governed by space in the material sense in that it is limited, and from a philosophical point of view any existence on earth is a voyage, not eternal but of limited extent. The artist who tries to capture the element of space in his composition, by recording or suggesting it, is almost attempting the impossible if he employs a *static* medium. Probably only ever-changing mobiles and

Giacomo Balla
(1871–1958)
Whirling motor-car
pastel
17½ × 22⅞ in (44 × 58 cm)
Marlborough Fine Art
London

space compositions and power-driven *kinetic* art can make us experience fully the sensation of space in art. The traditional artist, by contrast, often has to be content to illustrate the illusion of space by using oils on canvas, and it is interesting to consider how far he can hope to succeed when depicting a non-figurative theme, such as movement or force.

1920 Piet Mondrian
*Composition in grey, red,
yellow and blue*
39¼ × 39½ in
Tate Gallery
London

1971 Ilya Bolotowsky
Variation V
screenprint
London Arts Gallery

1924 Theo van Doesburg
Contra Composition
Gemeentemusea
Amsterdam

1968 Marcello Morandini
Development
wood sculpture
262×1·75×50 cm
private collection

Moholy-Nagy has been extensively cited as one of those who put the new concept of space into practice, but even earlier the Futurists, the Rayonists and the Constructivists felt the need for a fourth dimension in art, that is to say, space in the sense of movement.

Mario Sironi
Urban landscape
Galleria d'Arte Moderna
Milan

1962–63 Fritz Wotruba
Reclining figure
marble
77 × 161 × 53 cm
Wilhelm Lehmbruck Museum
Duisburg

Marinetti, in his Futurist Manifesto of 1909, announced a new beauty
created by machines or figures in motion, which gave rise to dynamic
sensation : the substance of objects was destroyed by movement
and light. Rayonism, created between 1911 and 1912 by Larionov,

Joan Miró (born 1893)
Woman and bird
oil on canvas
39½ × 25¾ in
London Arts Gallery

sought to go beyond the aims of Futurism by suggesting in paint the lapse of time and space – thus claiming a fourth dimension in art. These Rayonist paintings, with areas divided into flickering beams, are considered, alongside the more well-known paintings by Kandinsky, as some of the first truly abstract compositions ever created. Coined as an art term by Apollinaire, Orphism, from 1912, although mainly trying to enliven the restrained palette of Cubism, set out to search for dynamic space represented by vivid, coloured areas. Gabo and Pevsner were perhaps the first successful sculptors to translate the new Cubist concept of space into three-dimensional terms, thus giving it a new dimension of volume. In their basic aims they were closely related to Suprematism, 1913, founded by Malevich, who advocated the use of basic elements such as squares, triangles and circles, the true painterly elements, to create a new approach to aesthetic space. Moholy-Nagy, in his *New Vision* of 1928, was to inspire the artists and designers of the present day, and those teaching the new aesthetics of space. In 1925 El Lissitzky was to employ these principles in typography out of which, indirectly, Tschichold's *Neue Typographie* grew. The Dadaists of 1916 and the Surrealists of the 1920's, movements with their own theory of time and the co-incident, are at the other extreme; they are the representatives of the concept of *emotional* space. Incidentally, Arp, one of the early Dadaists, was between 1926 and 1930 a Surrealist, and in 1931 a member of the circle of *abstraction-création*, and, at the same time, he worked with Van Doesburg of *De Stijl*. There are dangers in too neatly pigeon-holing artists and movements.

1965–66 Hans Arp
Collage
private collection

1965–66 Edgar Mansfield
Binding
African native dyed red morocco
inlaid in natural dark brown,
lemon-yellow, yellow ochre and
two neutralized greens,
recessed in three depths

Composition = area + space

Space is the interval between areas. Both area and space make up a composition. The term composition is by no means confined to the visual arts. It can mean : the act of putting together ; the formation, construction ; the formation of words into a compound word ; the construction of sentences, the art of literary production ; the act, art, of composing music, a piece of music or writing ; the setting up of type ; the arrangement of the parts of a picture, etc. ; the thing composed, mixture.

The most obviously different types of composition in art are those that are *symmetrical* and those that are *asymmetrical* – but is a truly symmetrical composition really possible and aesthetically satisfactory ? Has it got enough dynamic quality to stir the senses of the spectator ? Even the most traditional art which appears symmetrical is often not entirely so. In this respect traditional art is just as modern as contemporary art. Although it is difficult to generalize, even in a classical composition great attention is paid to obtaining the right measure of symmetry and asymmetry. Consider Leonardo's *Last Supper*, painted between 1495 and 1497. The structure of the composition, i.e. the architectural properties of the interior and the position are entirely symmetrical, obeying proudly the recently discovered laws of perspective ; but in contrast, the language of hands swings above this symmetry to form a rhythm of never-ending 'togetherness', and this not only by the language of hands, but also by the direction of view, the treatment of figures and even of the drapery which are all depicted in forceful asymmetry. Analysing the

1495–97 Leonardo da Vinci
The last supper
detail
Santa Maria delle Grazie
Milan

1509–11 Raphael
St Paul preaching at Athens
detail from cartoon
Royal Collection
Victoria and Albert Museum
London

Pietro Cascella
Composition
sculpture
private collection

composition into basic areas and spaces will demonstrate this point
fully ; in fact, it will make Leonardo's work look like a modern
composition. An analysis of Raphael's *Cartoons* of 1509–11 will
result in the same kind of observation. In fact, this work has no static,
symmetrical background but a dynamic, asymmetrical structure and
composition.

1969 Lynn Chadwick
3 maquettes of Elektras
bronze
height 11¾, 31, 15½ in
Marlborough Fine Art
London

Com-position and leitmotiv

There has been discussion as to how far it is possible to differentiate between composition and structure. It is well known that Goethe, for instance, did not like the term composition at all. He would analyse it as *com-position*, demonstrating that it really describes the 'putting-together', and making work together objects placed in different positions, thus creating tension and interest. Goethe believed that every work of art is really a structure, even a work of music, which we, most naturally, call a composition (in fact this term was taken over by the visual arts from music). Following this way of thinking, it would be possible to claim that a work of music has really only one *leitmotiv,* one dominating main structure, and all the other elements are mere variations of this.

In the visual arts, the term 'composition' is more likely to occur in connexion with painting. 'Structure' refers more often to an object or a work of architecture and design which is conceived as a whole, serves basically one function, and provides one main facility to which all the others are related and co-ordinated.

Looking at the topic from this point of view, it is easy to understand that a painting or illustration is thought by the public primarily to tell a story, to report and to have going on in the different parts of the composition many 'happenings', a kind of *reportage*, be it in figurative or non-figurative style, or expressed in line, colour or texture. Those who are designing structures which are expected to provide shelter or to perform a service have to consider their practical

Roland Frey, Hermann Schröder,
Claus Schmidt
Hill for living
project for 46 homes in
one terraced-shaped building

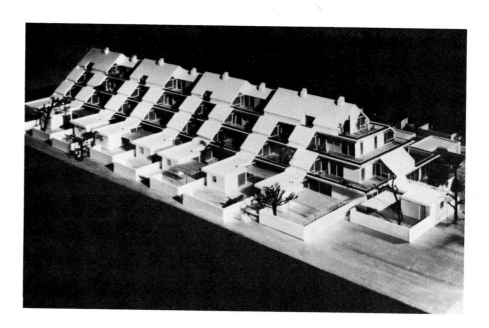

value and application. Sculpture, which has a supporting structure,
is more difficult to classify into either category. Perhaps more
definitely it belongs to the field of structure and leitmotiv, while the
term composition could be taken to mean the ever-changing visual
aspects that become apparent with the shifting position of the
observer. Sculpture, whether works chiselled from one block of
marble, cast into bronze in one working or built up in plaster to form
one item, is more obviously the result of one overall thought and of
one structure.

4th century B.C.
Votive relief
presentation to Artemis Bendis
of the torch passed from
horseman to horseman, in the
race run in her honour,
at the Piraeus
20½ × 33 in
British Museum
London

Baldassare Peruzzi
(1481–1536)
Analysis of proportions
British Museum
London

Timeless proportions?

The golden section has often been described as an absolute principle of composition, that is, one not only dominating the structure of nature and of living creatures, but also of art. But are there in art ideal proportions which can claim to be of eternal value? Can it be assumed that this mysterious proportion possesses some aesthetic virtue in itself, some hidden harmonic proportion in tune with the universe? Aesthetic concepts obey the laws of change, and therefore the validity and application of such a principle might be thought to be relatively limited. However, the golden section may easily be discovered in most works of art, architecture, and design. It can be found in Classical architecture, as well as in the works of the Romanesque period and the Italian Renaissance where it is used to articulate areas and to organize composition, intervals, and rhythm. In design and in the applied arts and crafts its presence can sometimes be detected. The golden section is the result of the search for good proportions and harmony by the application of the laws of geometry. This search can be traced back to the early days of Greek philosophy. The Middle Ages explored more fully the mysterious aspect of the laws of proportions, giving them almost a religious meaning. In the sixteenth century the golden section was often compared with the three components of the Trinity in a religious sense. Some have gone as far as to assert that the golden section can secure good proportions of height and width in matters as diverse as the two dimensions of a painting, a page of a book, a poster or leaflet, a window and a door, even of musical instruments, Gothic cathedrals, and the Egyptian pyramids. In more recent times, there has been an art movement called

1485–90 Leonardo da Vinci
*Human figure in a circle,
illustrating proportions*
pen and ink
34·3 × 24·5 cm
Galleria dell'Accademia
Venice

the *Section d'Or*. The name was coined in 1912 by the Parisian painter and graphic designer Jacques Villon. This group discussed the theory of Cubism, for the first time, with the founders of the theory, Gleizes and Metzinger, and with fellow artists, among them Picabia, Juan Gris, Léger, Delaunay, de la Fresnaye, Marcel Duchamp, Villon, Duchamp-Villon, and writers such as Jean Cocteau. They had 'borrowed' the idea of the golden section from the theories of Leonardo, which were now translated into new terms to explain the principles of Cubism, i.e. they were used to give aesthetic significance to geometry, and to divide the visual perception of an object into pyramids.

Though each generation looks at the aesthetics of art and design with its own eyes, though each generation has its favourite periods of the past, wanting, so to speak, to write its own interpretation and history of these subjects, there are, nevertheless, some basic principles that remain. There are some observations that can be generalized – dangerous as it may appear. The human body inspired the proportions of the golden section. The realization of this led to its application to works of architecture, sculpture, painting, inscriptions, manuscripts, works of printing, photography or graphic design. In all these disciplines proportions, once found in the human body, have been applied to satisfy the needs of the human race, as in purely functional objects such as doors, chairs and tables and also in works in the fine arts and in *objets d'art*. Beauty exists in these *proportions* – not necessarily in the elements themselves, but in their relationships.

1968 Josef Bauer
Modules
fibreglass, wood
height 196 cm
Galerie im Griechenbeisl
Vienna :
proportions in modern art

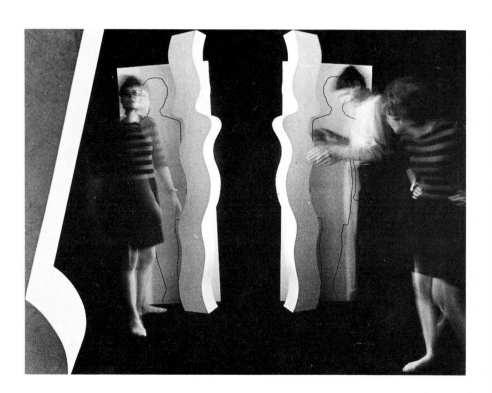

Examples of such relationships are one part of a finger and another, all fingers and the hand, and the arm and body ; or an eye to a nose and a mouth to the whole head. The most widely adopted system of proportions certainly *is* the so-called golden section.

Modules for the future

The golden section is one of the basic guides to the attainment of good proportions by mathematical means. For the same reason the golden section is perhaps sometimes called the *golden mean*. It must, however, be said that all geometrical means are only attempts to find a beginning, an inspiration for an artistic or a design activity : they cannot replace the creative mind nor take over the artist's work but only support it. The proportions of the golden section are based on the following principle : the smaller dimension stands to the greater dimension as the greater stands to the whole and undivided dimension. The greater is called *major*, the smaller *minor*. The *Laumé* numerical system – 3 : 5, 5 : 8, 8 : 13, 13 : 21, 21 : 34, and so on – approaches most accurately these proportions.

This system can be applied in fields ranging from typographic design, stamp design, stage, interior, and industrial design to the majestic proportions of architecture and functional engineering. The golden section is also used of course in the fine arts. For centuries painters have not painted the horizon exactly in the centre, which would look unexciting, but consciously or unconsciously in a position suggested by the golden mean. In design a variety of experiments, or actual commissions, can be based on these proportions, e.g. the grouping of elements such as type or quads, triangles, circles and rules. In typographic design this comes quite naturally as many elements of typography already contain the stamp of the golden section : the relationship of ascenders and descenders to x-height, size of type to leading, size of book type to type for marginal notes, size of headline to

Ivor Kamlish
Symbol
the proportions of which are
clearly based on a module

initial and the proportions of the type area, width to height, or type area to paper size. Creating within the rules of the golden section does not necessarily mean being restricted to a symmetrical design. In fact, the rules inspire an asymmetrical approach because proportions of irregular intervals lend themselves easily and perfectly to a similar irregular grouping rather than to an arrangement around some central axis.

For the architect, but also for the artist and designer, the *Modulor* of Le Corbusier may be interesting, revealing and useful. Le Corbusier, early in his career, fully realized that in modern architecture and in the design of any object for functional use, such as chairs and tables, there was a need for modules and similar working aids. Of course, he is not the only member of the modern movement to have recognized this, nor should it be forgotten that for centuries generations of architects had felt the need for a module. It is definitely established that, for instance, in Romanesque architecture 'units' were used by the master builders to measure and indeed outline their plans for a workable system in the construction of a church or a secular building. They would simply 'count' in units, long before the semi-anonymous master builders of the Gothic period found more ambitious systems of architectural planning, and thus succeeded in providing a functional structure for their cathedral-buildings with spires of daring height (the highest one, Ulm, *c.*528 feet). These same medieval builders, still believing in some mysterious power, sometimes ran away overnight to escape from the terrible and

1946 Le Corbusier
Modulor
original sketch
private collection

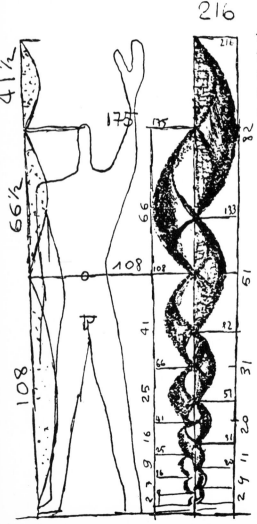

frightening thought that their constructions might collapse – as, in fact, many Gothic spires have, centuries after they were put up. The architects of the Renaissance, such as Vitruvius and especially Sebastiano Serlio, searched into the antique past in their aim to renew the principles of the Classical orders of architecture and to find new modules for their work. The Italian Sebastiano Serlio, from 1542 court architect at Fontainebleau, is perhaps the most prominent theorist whose theses, published in the years after 1537, were widely translated into most European languages including French, Dutch, English, and German.

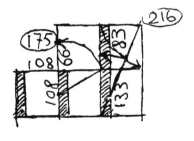

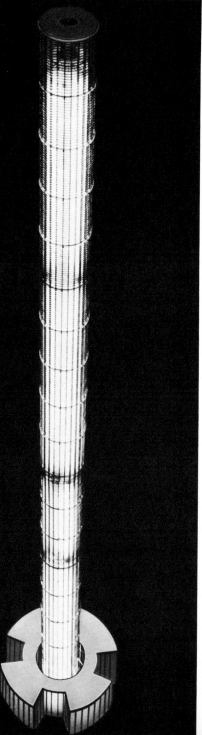

1965 Robert Gabriel
Tower city for 25,000 persons
planned to be 356 stories above
and 16 stories beneath the earth

Le Corbusier, in basing his system of modules on the human body, linked up also with the ideas of Renaissance artists such as Leonardo and Dürer, not for the purpose of following traditional perspective or traditional orders or well-known systems of proportions, but to provide a new system for living. He followed these principles throughout his career, proving that it is quite possible to vary ideas and approaches almost without limitation, while still working within one system of modules. In his *Unité* at Marseilles of 1945, for instance, which as the name suggests, provides living space for a community (of some 6000) 'united' under one roof, basic modules are used in endless variety, for the height of ceilings, doors, areas for household activities, recreation, and social activities.

The pioneers of the modern movement in art, design, and architecture have inspired their colleagues of today who, more than any generation before, are involved in working out modules to satisfy the demand for prefabricated units and many other mass-produced products. These modules in their turn may one day be the only way to provide for the living needs of an ever-growing world population. To find modules or any system of units or proportions that can help to do this aesthetically, as effectively as possible, within the well-known economic limitations of any project, should be welcomed, since modules are, in Einstein's phrase, 'a scale of proportions whereby the bad is made more difficult and the good easier'.

Creative light and colour

Reflection of light
enhanced by the camera,
photographed by the author

exhibited 1843
William Turner
Light and Colour
(Goethe's theory) :
the morning after the deluge :
Moses writing the Book of Genesis
31 × 31 in
Tate Gallery
London

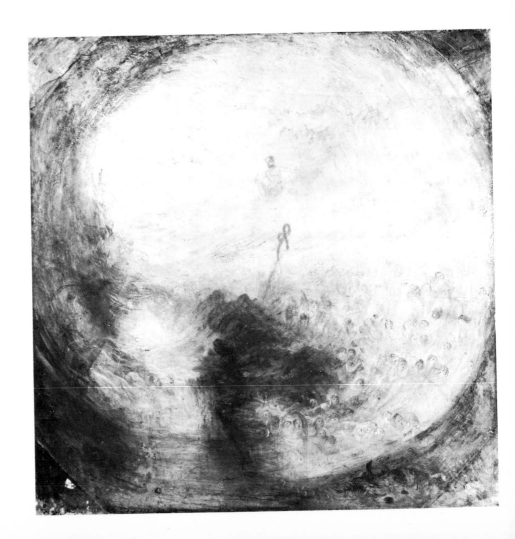

To see light and colour

Light is an element of the universe. Only by the existence of light are we able to see and be aware of colour. We can do this only because the human eye has developed to a stage where it can distinguish and 'specify' colour. The animal eye is different. It is well known that some animals have a different, often less refined, scale of colour perception than human beings – it is the same in the case of the acoustic perception of animals – and, of course, there are colour-blind people who have only a limited range of colour perception. The primitive human eye may have had a much less developed perception scale, and it was perhaps able to distinguish only between stronger or weaker radiation. There must have been many stages of evolution, over millions of years, to attain the normal perceptive quality of the twentieth-century eye. It could be that at one period of life on earth no living being could perceive the differentiated frequencies which make it possible for the human eye today to register *chromatic* colours. The eye, which today perceives the different rays which build up to 'chromatic perception', may have been content, in primitive days, to register only black and white and tones of grey, the so-called *achromatic* colours, giving an image comparable to a black and white photograph. The contemporary eye has kept this latter capacity when perceiving these 'colourless colours', as achromatic colours are sometimes called.

It is difficult to explain exactly how visual colour perception works. We are able to see when our senses have been stimulated – which happens when white light, broken into various wave-lengths, reaches

1934
Robert Delaunay
Endless rhythm

our eyes. These different wave-lengths result from reflection or refraction. We see not just tones of grey but different hues, or colours, which complete our perception of the shapes of objects and make them more alive and more detailed, giving them personality, and properties such as warmth and coldness. Sometimes it is said that a certain person's eye is quick, or quicker than another's. In fact, it can be assumed that, although there might be differences in the physical ability of reaction, the eye is, in general, a quite neutral instrument. It *records* events. It works in close contact with other factors by which it is stimulated. Fortunately for the 'aesthetic vision' – i.e. the propensity to know in advance or to make up one's mind what to look for or to recognize characteristics when they appear before the pupil – this sense need not be entirely inborn : it can be educated to reach a higher standard of recognition.

1958 Henry Moore
Reclining figure
Unesco Building
Paris

Sunset at Bagno Paradiso
photographed by the author

1970 Marcello Salvadori
Eclipse no 2
phase 1 and 2
kinetic construction
19 × 18 × 8 in

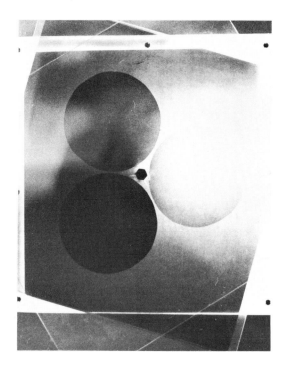

Expressive light

Light is an essential part of life which we notice most when it is absent. We usually take the presence of light for granted and are never really concerned about it; we have to see light in an unusual connexion to become conscious of it. A beautiful sunset, the reflection of light on the sea, lightning, all make us fully aware of the existence of this element of nature. Our attention is enhanced, however, when we see light in its own right as a means of artistic expression, as in the theatre and cinema. In the theatre, special effects are 'designed' with different lighting and there is no doubt that the effective lighting of an interior or of an exterior, e.g. a garden, a park, architecture in *son et lumière*, or of an exhibition or display, raises the quality of the object and draws attention to it. Photography and the cinema would not be possible without light. The reflective qualities of light and colour are well known to the artist and explored by him. In nature the reflection of light produces colour. There is certainly a difference in the impression gained of a landscape or townscape according to weather conditions: sun, snow, time of day and season. The shiny surface of objects and materials, e.g. gold and inlays, has been explored by designers and craftsmen for generations and the contemporary designer exploits them for purposes of mass production and in the creation of industrial products. In designing, the ability to blend light and colour with form is often crucial. Warm and cool colours are often 'combined' by light. The reflection of different lights, as practised in the theatre in order to create a third, new colour or shade of colour, has the same theoretical basis as the artist's use of colour.

Movement and light
the giant wheel
at the Vienna Prater

Movement, sound and music

The expressive quality of light is often accompanied by movement and sound as in dance, the theatre, opera, and the cinema, while the emotional quality of colour has been compared with music. Light is used creatively in works of painting, drawing, and sculpture. Its application goes back to the very origins of art. The school of the Impressionists, for whom the rendering of the effects of light was an essential principle, had its forerunners in Daumier and La Tour.

Modern art has brought about the dramatic use of light as a means of artistic expression in its own right. In kinetic sculpture, light modulators and mobile constructions create ever-changing patterns by the controlled application of light, although the final art product and image is often left to the laws of coincidence. Modern life has given light innumerable applications : in entertainment, information and propaganda.

Erich Schulz-Anker, art director
Wolfgang Körber, designer
Typorama
perpetual kinetic composition
for exhibition stand
of D Stempel AG type foundry
at the Frankfurt Book Fair

c.1814–16
Francisco José de Goya
The convention of the
Compania de Filipinas
Nationalgalerie
Berlin

1823 Caspar David Friedrich
Moon rising over the sea
Nationalgalerie
Berlin

*c.*1852 Eugène Delacroix
Rape of women by Turks
oil on canvas
54 × 65·5 cm
Kunsthalle
Mannheim

*c.*1865 Honoré Daumier
Collectors of etchings
oil on wood
27 × 36 cm
Kunsthalle
Mannheim

1874 Claude Monet
Seine bridge near Argenteuil
oil on canvas
60 × 81·3 cm
Bayerische Staatsgemäldesammlungen
Munich

Sunny scene at Barcelona with light filtering through the trees in an impressionist manner, photographed by the author

Edvard Munch
(1863–1944)
Composition
with maximum of
light contrast

1970 Bruno Munari
Xerografia
light composition with innumerable
xerographic variations
of one word
Rank Xerox
Milan

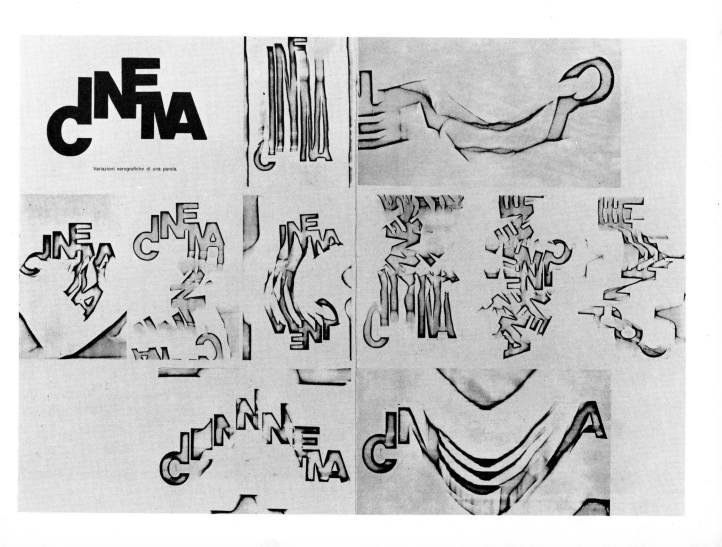

Variazioni xerografiche di una parola.

Multi-storey block of flats
colour rhythm as an important
element of design :
plastic parts supplied in
different shades of Hostalit-Z
by Farbwerke Hoechst

Colour rhythm

In designing, formal values – size, form, and material – are more often than not emphasized consciously and planned by logical thinking ; colour is perhaps more frequently used unconsciously and applied and employed by intuition, an inborn sense of colour. The human eye is automatically attracted by forceful colours because the eye is not accustomed to seeing them on a large scale. Nature provides mainly soothing colours such as green and brown on a large scale and shows more brilliant colours such as yellow and red only sparingly.
Colour can also be an important element of design in creating rhythm. Sometimes this colour rhythm will be 'hidden', sometimes it will be so placed as to attract attention, by letting colour fall at an obvious place or in an obvious connexion or composition. In other cases, colour might be symbolically and psychologically adjusted to the intended planning of an area or a volume. It plays an essential part in creating rhythm, especially in primitive art and in Western art before the discovery of perspective in the Renaissance – and indeed in modern art and architecture which often turn their backs on ornament and figurative presentation. In modern architecture and product design, for example, colour has often taken the place of ornament and classical systems of creating rhythm and is frequently used to create rhythm in its own right. The area, which was fully discovered by modern painting, is also of great importance in the creation of rhythm by colour in contemporary architecture. Gropius, Rietveld, Van Doesburg, Mies van der Rohe, and Le Corbusier are among those who have achieved both harmony and surprise by blending areas of pure colour into architectural rhythm and structure.

Colour symbolism

Since the dawn of the human race, a symbolic meaning has been attached to most of the principal colours. According to tradition, *black* stands for mourning in most Western societies but for rejoicing in some African and Eastern civilizations, where the colour of mourning is white. This shows that colour symbolism exists often by tradition and association. It is therefore very difficult to judge whether the symbolic properties and associations normally attached to a certain colour are truly the result of impulses, giving rise to a reaction or feeling, and not just faithful adherence to a well-established tradition. In most Western societies *white* stands for innocence and purity. In tropical countries the reflective quality of white and other very light colours is recognized as a protection against the heat of the sun and often the colour tradition of these countries is in contrast to Western traditions as a result of functional considerations.

Red is a colour that is associated with strong emotions and, paradoxically, can be quite contradictory in nature. Red is the colour of love and also the colour of unity, but it has been used, by succeeding generations, as the colour of revolution. By its strong intensity, red is most useful to attract the attention of the public. This might be the reason that red stands for danger, rather than the fact that if one runs into danger an accident may result in the loss of blood. The unity symbolism of red might well be related to the sentiment of brotherhood and blood relationship. The short-wave or high intensity of red which causes a quick reaction in the onlooker is used a great deal for purely utilitarian purposes such as to indicate, in a logical way, the most

Marianne Werefkin
Shingle making
mixed technique
105 × 80 cm
Städtisches Museum
Wiesbaden

By long established association
we can well imagine the pure
and brilliant colours of this
Fauve painting

important part of a machine, e.g. the push button to operate it, or to stop it, or to attract attention in other ways, e.g. the rear lights of a car, traffic lights, fire engines or (in Britain) pillar boxes. In contrast, red may be used to enhance richness and warmth as in carpets or furniture.

Warm *yellow,* the colour of gold, of the sun and of the Creation (in the vocabulary of the painter Van Gogh) symbolizes joy, richness and glory and music in a major key. In contrast, pale yellow, closely associated with pale green, may stand for envy and greed but, above all, such a yellow indicates cowardice. Emotionally, a 'nasty' green represents also envy and jealousy, as expressed in the phrase 'green with envy'. *Green* is, however, traditionally the colour of hope, based on the relaxing properties of nature, and was probably maintained by a rural population moving into urban society for exactly this reason. The traditional use of green as a soothing colour in institutions such as hospitals and schools is certainly not without reason, because green is the colour of life, youth, growth, and health.

Blue is considered the colour of the intellect, a fresh, clear, logical attitude, and there is good reason to suggest that this could be related to the eternal quality of the sky and enables a person to think with a clear mind. A combination of greens and blues could be ideal to establish colour schemes which provide the right atmosphere for relaxed thinking. Of course, the tone value and intensity within a colour are important in creating the precise symbolic colour meaning. *Violet* is said to be unbearable in larger areas, standing for repentance,

1936 Alexej von Jawlensky
Restrained passion
oil on cardboard
27 × 20 cm
Städtisches Museum
Wiesbaden

A further stage of abstraction
supported by strong symbolic
colours in a Fauve painting

but, in the current trends of fashion, it is used to a larger extent, and made more acceptable to the human eye, by adding white to it – thus transforming it into a soft lilac. Violet and purple have been symbolically used by the church and by sovereigns to stress and 'support' their power by exposing to their subjects a colour that is so stirring that it must be noticed. The impact state ceremony still makes upon modern society is perhaps partly explained by the display of colours that both express glory (brilliant yellow) and evoke emotion (violet and purple).

Basically, the colour pageantry of both state and church go back to remote times when sovereignty could communicate to a predominantly illiterate public only in terms of symbolism such as heraldry, the 'shorthand' and forerunner of verbal inscriptions. In fact, this colour association goes back to the life of primitive people who saw in colour the great powers of good and evil; there were colours that could heal the sick while others would bring success or disaster. *Colour combinations* are also not only a question of convention but of habit, often of quickly created habits as can be observed in the ever-changing combination of colours in the field of fashion – the attitude that 'blue and green should not be seen' is hardly valid today and Picasso's revolution in combining browns and blues in his post-Cubist period is now fully accepted in fashion and interior design.

Psychological and optical observations

Malevich believed strongly in
a colour symbolism with white
standing for purity,
blue for eternity,
black for night and
brilliant colours for dynamism

Contemporary painting has to no small extent contributed towards a rediscovery of colour and its psychological power, and this is also reflected in the graphic arts : consider the use of colour in advertising. Colour has in more than one sense been compared with music. In the same way that a series of notes must be selected and arranged to produce a piece of music, colour is a kind of basic material that needs combination and composition to gain an artistic life of its own. The principles of harmony that satisfy the aesthetic demands of the human eye have sometimes been described as colour sense, or 'colour-culture'. Although this sense exists to a certain extent in the majority of people, it needs developing and refining if it is to be used successfully in an artistic career.

Opinion on a particular colour will naturally vary according to the extent to which the colour reacts on the individual. Even the opinion of experts differs greatly, for instance, on the question as to whether black and white are colours in the usual sense. Professor Ostwald describes them as colourless colours, while Kandinsky does not consider them as colours at all. But on comparing the two it will be noticed that white appears much warmer than black. Symbolically and scientifically analysed, white also reveals an 'ascending' and black a 'descending' tendency. Black and white are the poles of absolute lightness while yellow and blue are the poles of colour lightness, i.e. brightness and intensity.

Marcello Morandini
a group of modern experiments
all showing the weight of colour
at the 34th Biennale di Venezia

The term *weight of colour* is in fact based on such observation though, like all abstract terms, it is not measurable. It can only be established by feeling and, of course, the weight of a colour will depend on the area occupied by an individual colour. There is also the problem of colour and tone value. Experiments with rectangular areas of black and white of the same size clearly demonstrate the tone value of colours. A piece of grey placed in turn on a white and then on a black background gives the illusion of different tone values. Similarly red on a yellow background appears dark, whereas the same red on a blue background looks considerably brighter and warmer. The tone value of a colour depends largely on its surroundings, and it is important to distinguish between a colour as such and its apparent tone value, the latter being a relative term. The degree of brightness of a colour and its tone value do not always correspond to each other. Not only the optical appearance but also the character of a colour can be varied by its background. A colour, except a very dull one, looks most intense on a dark background, e.g. red lettering on black. The most compact impression of a colour is achieved by putting it on white. All colours appear darker on a white background, whereas light colours are invariably strengthened by a black background. Printed against a white background, a colour must not be too light or its legibility is bound to suffer ; yellow lettering on white is literally outshone by its background, but the same yellow lettering on black will prove most effective. Of course, where functional aspects need not be considered, as in painting, the combination of yellow on white might be ideal to convey a certain mood. The legibility of printed type can be greatly improved by a clear distinction between display colour and base colour. The display colour should be a bright one, the base colour, forming the bulk of the text, should be printed in a comparatively neutral colour such as black or grey, a very deep blue or any colour that has been dulled by adding a touch of another.

Means to emphasize form

The property of a colour in supporting and emphasizing form in order to express a certain mood more efficiently could be described as the 'temperament' of a colour. The creative artist certainly makes use of this 'complementary' treatment of form and colour and more often unconsciously than consciously. A pleasant, round, warm shape, can be successfully emphasized by an equally warm colour such as red or orange. In publicity a warm colour temperament is considered a good means of attracting attention. In contrast a cold, icy, sharp, pushing shape, certainly active but perhaps unpleasant and evoking only feelings of respect and not of warmth, could be psychologically emphasized by a cold colour such as a shade of blue. This theory of colour temperament can be applied historically to different periods. The Gothic period, which advocated 'restraint from lust', almost apologizing for the existence of the pleasures of life and living, frequently used cold colours to underline the angular, spiky, and sharp forms of architecture, sculpture, and lettering. By contrast, the Baroque period, playing cheerfully with the effects of light, gave the voluminous and swinging forms of architecture, sculpture and lettering an unmatchable *éclat* by the brilliance of optimistic, *joie de vivre* colours.

The effects of transparency of light and colour are explored by artists and architects in many fields, e.g. in fenestration, or to expose a kind of atmospheric perspective. Advancing and receding tones serve to create the feeling of space. The plastic effect of light is well known, in 'modelling' to the observer the intended appearance of a work of

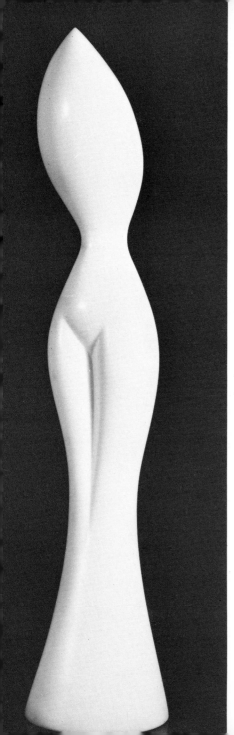

1963 Hans Arp
Torse accentué
white marble
26½ × 6½ × 6½ in
London Arts Gallery :
the plastic effect of
light explored

art or a product of design. Experiments have been made with abstract lighting. The painters of light, the Impressionists and their forerunners, were followed by those who assembled physical and visual material, thus creating tonal and textural relationship by an ever-changing use of light. Homogeneous materials, such as stone, metal or wood in sculpture or terra-cotta in a vase, are made more attractive to the eye and the other senses by using light effects to interplay with form.

Here are a few observations that may help to train one's sense of light and colour. It is quite revealing to find out about the relationship between light and colour on the one hand, and formal values, such as (1) line, or (2) area, space, composition, or (3) texture, surface, structure, on the other. It would be useful to select say three works by prominent artists and examine how they use light and colour. Even simple and effortless, but active, observation can help. Looking at fashions could enable one to find out about chromatic and achromatic colours as well as revealing tone value, brightness and intensity. Even the dullest formal fashions demonstrate the numerous different greys which lie between the poles of white and black and the subtle contrast between warm and cold greys.

Colour experiments are invaluable experience for the future artist and designer in satisfying technical needs and will assist the development of creative ability ; but only by a spontaneous method can colour experiments become a means of true artistic expression, a means of true colour emotion.

Structure, surface, texture

Structure, surface and texture,
haphazard in arrangement,
photographed by the author

1954–57 Naum Gabo
Sculpture
for the department store
de Bijenkorf
Rotterdam

98

Interchangeable terms?

Structure is defined in the Oxford dictionary as : the way in which a thing holds together, the supporting framework or essential parts, a building or any complex whole . . . *structural*=of the essential framework. From Latin *struo*=to build.

Surface is given as : the outside of a body, the limits terminating a solid, outward aspect of material or immaterial thing, what is apprehended of something upon a casual view or consideration, e.g., has a smooth, uneven surface ; presents large surface to view . . .

Texture is described as : arrangement of threads in texture fabric, degree of openness or closeness in a surface or substance when felt or looked at, e.g. cloth, skin, wood ; of loose, fine, coarse texture ; arrangement of constituent parts, structure, e.g. of skin, rock, literary work ; representation of surface of objects in works of art ; Biology : tissue, structure of this. From Latin *textura*=as text.

These dictionary definitions indicate how the educated layman will see these terms. For the artist, designer and all who are visually involved, texture, surface, and structure have a definite, special meaning which relates to their creative activities. But even for them it is highly useful to study these terms first of all in their general sense. The artist and designer who wants truly to understand texture, surface, and structure has to adopt, at the beginning of his studies, a child's attitude in order to regain tactile abilities which the average person loses when growing up – especially those members of a

1925 Naum Gabo
*Construction in space
balanced on two points*
50 × 26½ in
Yale Art Gallery

Bridge
river Elbe
near Lauenburg

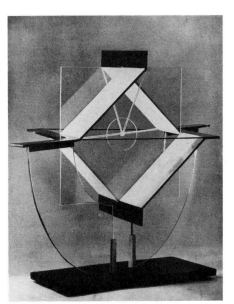

highly developed civilization. In contrast, people still living close to
nature normally have basic senses that are far more highly developed,
e.g. a feeling for a duration of time or good orientation. Conventionally
we speak of the five senses : we can see, hear, smell, taste, and touch.
The sensations caused by touch and vision are transmitted to us
either by exterior or interior impulses. Our whole life is a development
of such experiences, starting with the baby being fed by its mother,

1925 Antoine Pevsner
Round construction
bronze
45 × 48 cm

1942–3 Naum Gabo
Linear construction
plastic with plastic thread
13¾ × 13¾ in
Tate Gallery
London

1967
The 61st Rhine bridge
'the slanting ropes bridge'
520 m long, 36 m wide
Bonn

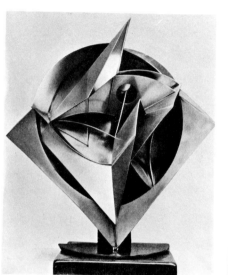

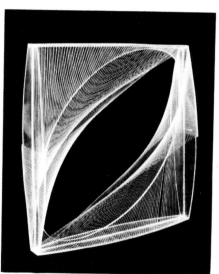

tasting food, touching toys. Therefore, in artistic development this first-hand experience should exist and indeed the student should be trained fully to build up a broad creative outlook rather than to be content with second-hand experience from reading and tuition. Paradoxical as it sounds, it is often only by going back to early or primitive sources that truly individual aesthetic expression can be found.

before 1651
Diego Rodriguez Velázquez
The toilet of Venus
'Rokeby Venus'
c.48¼ × 69¾ in
detail
National Gallery
London

The drama of structure and texture

In this section we shall consider structure, how a study of nature and aesthetics can help the artist and designer and, in particular, the possibilities and limitations dictated by purpose and material. Furthermore we shall examine structure and ornament, pattern derived from nature, and pattern based on function. It is the designer's business to establish structure within his visual world, to find out how structure works.

There is structure that evokes speed. There is structure that makes objects optically smaller or bigger, narrower or wider, as applied in product design, fashions, architecture. There is structure that is expressive and evokes powerful feelings, e.g. those experienced when standing underneath the Eiffel tower or a huge modern building or construction or scaffolding. There is disguised structure such as can sometimes be found in painting, where intermediate shadowy tones replace a sharp contour line, as in the *Rokeby Venus* by Velázquez. Naturally in modern painting and especially in non-figurative work disguised structure exists to a much greater extent. There is also unconscious structure and texture in some works of modern art in the form of accidental techniques. The simplest way of studying texture and structure is first of all to arrange material of the same kind in a composition and later to combine several kinds of materials and structure.

There are many ways of analysing and using texture. Nature reveals the texture of things growing. The architect incorporates texture into

1834–
John Constable
*A woman by an old willow tree
at Hamm, Surrey*
pen and bistre ink
9¼ × 5½ in (23·5 × 14 cm)
Victoria and Albert Museum
London

structure. Le Corbusier's monastery at La Tourette is a good example of using or rather leaving texture 'impressed' by nature, namely the wood grain made on the concrete surface of walls by the shoring. The industrial designer uses texture as an integral part of the product. The illustrator creates contours and outlines by assembling lines and scribbles. In painting, paint itself creates texture in patches of light and shade or where edges of forms merge into one another or into the tone of the background. Such painterly techniques are to be found in works ranging from Titian and Rembrandt to modern action painting and tachism. Botticelli and Michelangelo are among the least painterly of painters.

The apprehension of the underlying structure of a work of art, whether modern or traditional, makes demands on the spectator. Of course, a certain mystery can remain. Not everything has to be discussed and analysed, a great deal can be achieved by feeling things and by reacting to them spontaneously. The same is true when the designer selects his textures : a little theory is needed, but the most important is good taste and *Einfühlung*, i.e. sympathetic understanding of visual effects and material properties.

Nature sets an outstanding example by demonstrating functional structure in manifold and admirable ways. Functional considerations always seem to be decisive in the development of a natural structure. These structural properties can, in a special way, inspire the architect in his task of providing shelter for man. A comprehensive study of the

1957–60 Le Corbusier
La Tourette
near Lyon

1968 Max Ernst
Collage
18½×15½ in
London Arts Gallery

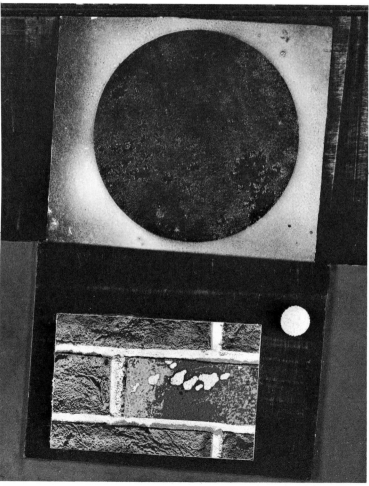

1961 Pier Luigi Nervi
Palace of labour
hall for international
exhibition
Turin

needs and habits of people will provide him with the information
necessary to plan and create structures that are efficient and
convenient. Eclectic or derivative architecture is inordinately
concerned with a representative facade, often neglecting the interior
grouping and 'leaving over' oddly shaped rooms – while good

1961 Pier Luigi Nervi
Palace of labour
hall for international
exhibition
Turin

contemporary architecture relies on functional structure, where the interior must be as aesthetically acceptable as the exterior. The beehive is an example of the 'architecture' of animals, but its structure never varies, is never open to choice. It is the privilege of the human being to create his own environment.

1962 David Stanfield
Poster
Council of Industrial Design
London

Visual relationships are not the only aspect of design – although in the fine arts they are perhaps more important than anything else. In design, structure is paramount. Architecture, and industrial design, have to be functional in the first instance, come what may – otherwise a building, a bridge, a chair might just collapse, or a product or machine might not work. In two-dimensional work this does not occur, but where any kind of functional structure is involved, structure is at the very heart of the problem. Perhaps it is for this reason that the designing of non-structural but predominantly visual material such as graphics or typography or wallpaper was until a few decades ago more often called commercial *art* and not *design* ('commercial' merely emphasizing the distinction between fine and applied art). In sculpture, structural relation only supports physically the visual relation, in other words, makes sure that the work of art gets physical and material 'support'. Even a painting, in physical terms colour applied to a surface, could not exist without a physical structure such as the canvas and the supporting frame.

It is perhaps best to discuss here only the structural aspects and relationships of truly or predominantly functional design, such as architecture, furniture, product-engineering and industrial design. Here, related structure is absolutely *objective*, dependent mainly on factual data such as the supporting capacity of a material – while, in contrast, the visual excitement created by it is *subjective*, i.e. dependent on the reaction of the observer to aesthetic properties.

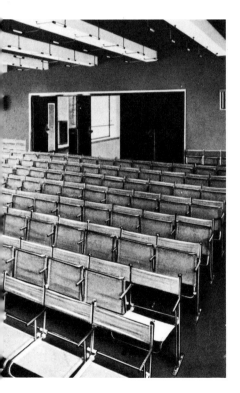

In the field of furniture, for instance, early consideration was given to the artistic aspect. It is unwise to call it the 'design' aspect because some antique furniture is certainly more enjoyable to look at than to sit on, and often little thought was given by the designer to storage capacity. This does not mean that good antique furniture cannot teach us a great deal about aesthetics. The exact opposite is true. We can learn much about materials and proportions and come to appreciate the historical and sentimental associations.

Furniture in the Gothic period certainly exhibited a structure that was functional although, with a few exceptions, it was not yet movable (or mobile, to trace the origin of the French *meuble*, which expresses furniture in the modern sense) but rather 'built-in' — an idea that is taken up again more and more by contemporary designers. The craftsman was the only one to decide about structure and visual appeal. In the Renaissance and early Baroque periods, great artists were employed who knew how to guide the craftsman. In Rococo and neo-Classical furniture the craftsman often became only the right hand of the artist who now developed new ideas of over-all decoration including furniture of the same style. The Victorian period found the craftsman using partly machine-produced elements and sometimes completely machine-produced furniture in 'new' materials such as *papier mâché.* These often had elaborate patterning where an honest structure was hidden by an historically false exterior. Only in our century does the designer, now fully established to create for and guide mass production, give serious thought to functional structure and

1959 Pier Luigi Nervi and
Annibale Vitellozzi
Palazzetto dello sport
Rome

1959 Pier Luigi Nervi and
Annibale Vitellozzi
Palazzetto dello sport
Rome

visually related structure before starting to design. Special ergonomic experimental units have even been developed to test the sitting, lying, or standing habits of people before a chair, a table, or a hospital bed is designed.

Minster
Freiburg

Residential towers
Hamburg
project

To create a well-related structure that works, a really good designer
is needed. Any structure has a system, except as used in the fine arts
where no rational function is attempted. An analysis of a chair or a
table or, at a more ambitious level, the structure of a Gothic tower or

1925 Mies van der Rohe
The Barcelona chair
Council of Industrial Design
London

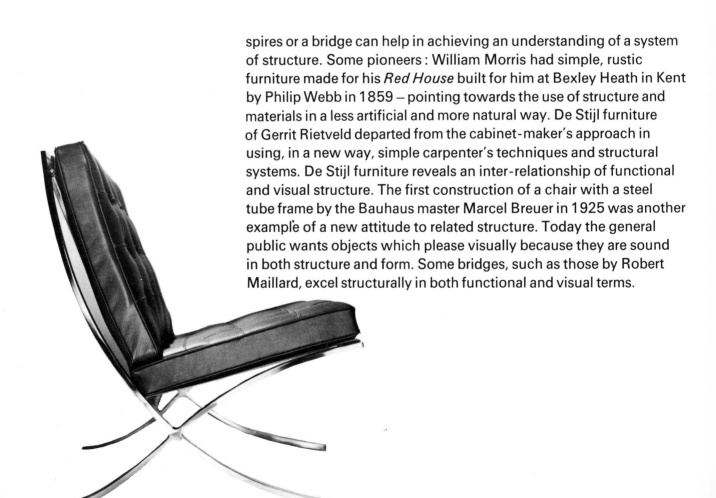

spires or a bridge can help in achieving an understanding of a system of structure. Some pioneers : William Morris had simple, rustic furniture made for his *Red House* built for him at Bexley Heath in Kent by Philip Webb in 1859 – pointing towards the use of structure and materials in a less artificial and more natural way. De Stijl furniture of Gerrit Rietveld departed from the cabinet-maker's approach in using, in a new way, simple carpenter's techniques and structural systems. De Stijl furniture reveals an inter-relationship of functional and visual structure. The first construction of a chair with a steel tube frame by the Bauhaus master Marcel Breuer in 1925 was another example of a new attitude to related structure. Today the general public wants objects which please visually because they are sound in both structure and form. Some bridges, such as those by Robert Maillard, excel structurally in both functional and visual terms.

1968 Jean Dubuffet
Buste effigique
painted styrofoam
42 × 22 × 22 in
London Arts Gallery

Man feels form
or the touch of quality

There are things we like touching and things we dislike touching – we react to them spontaneously by saying 'nice' or 'horrible'. By creative use, the designer experiences materials very closely. He will discover properties and impressions to which he had previously not paid any attention. Using material either in manual craftsmanship or in industrial design or in designing for the machine, or for factory production, he will also find out more about the tectonic qualities of the available materials and indeed their most economic, functional, and aesthetic use. It is for these reasons that modern art education suggests, besides visual, creative and intellectual training, the direct contact with the working-tools of the craftsman and experimental work in which the student has to operate machines which the factory worker would use in executing his design. Tactile exercises with materials will help the student to become aware of the properties of texture and surface. A so-called *touch book*, a book containing numerous diverse materials, helps the student in tactile experiments just as direct contact with colour helps him visually. A summary of all these experiences will directly help the student to design in a more realistic way and, indirectly perhaps, to express himself with greater ease in visual terms.

Most people will only be convinced of the justification of such exercises if this practical application is made clear to them in terms of practical designing or in terms of economy and profit or a better sales appeal which helps in marketing a product. Some examples : one of the oldest markets involving products with tactile properties is in the world of publishing. Editors know why they ask the designer *and*

Erich Aurich
Binding
painted texture

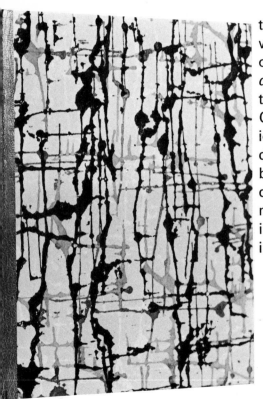

the book-binder, to find a presentation that the public will not only want to see and read but also to touch – as the touch of quality is an old-established hall-mark of a well-produced book, especially of a *de luxe* edition. The same principle of quality of touch is applied by the manufacturers to wrappers for chocolate, or to bottles for Champagne and Chianti. The sense of touch is employed to help identify a product or to indicate where to open a package. The designer of containers uses indentations to indicate where a part must be pressed to open a packet correctly, e.g. cigarette packets, detergent packets. The touch quality of wool, silk, a good brush, a soft mattress are explored by advertising copy-writers who make the imagination of the public travel and create a 'dream-demand', an irrational longing for these products.

Fiera del Bianco
poster
La Rinascente
Milan

Alexander Cozens
(1752–97)
Study of sky no 4
with landscape
pencil and brown wash
on varnished paper
8⅝×12¼ in (21·8×31 cm)
Royal Academy of Arts
London

Contrast of visual texture

The term *visual texture* is perhaps best described as a texture we can see, which invites us to touch it physically or at least 'lovingly' with our eyes, or in other words which produces by its texture a visual sensation. This could be equally the case with a work of sculpture, of architecture, with interior design, furniture, ceramics, a product of industrial design or, of course, when texture occurs in nature. The best example of visual texture is the sky, an ever-changing pattern of light, which we are obviously unable to touch. Sky texture often creates the sensation of speed, the kinetic quality of a fourth dimension, when the clouds are coming and going – but a static quality when they do not seem to move. In looking at the sky it may be assumed that, whatever is seen, it is not substance but merely impressions of light in space. Even the sky, however, gets misty, dull, covered or blurred at times, not giving the impression of a blue surface at all. The best kind of *visual* texture is created when it is closely related to *tactile* surface properties, and it is not without good reason that terms, explaining typical properties of visual texture, are related to those dealing with physical experiences of contrasts such as hard and soft, rough and smooth. Other terms in the field of visual textures describe properties only in the visual sense, terms such as dull and shiny, opaque and transparent, and metallic in contrast to anything that is soft and inviting. The artist and designer will explore these properties and emphasize them wherever possible, by shape and form, by techniques and composition.

1828 William Turner
East Cowes Castle
watercolour
5½ × 7 7/16 in (13·3 × 18·8 cm)
British Museum
London

Textural properties are explored in most art forms. This is the case not only in painting, as in tachism or action painting – where texture is explored for texture's sake and texture is made an art form in its own right – but in almost any field of art and design. Perhaps it is more often the case in pre-Renaissance, i.e. pre-perspective art forms and again in modern art. But painting is not possible without the foundations of texture that often assumes a meaning only within a composition. Texture can express so much and can so underline and support, that the atmosphere of a work of art, however classical it might be, often depends on it. In more recent art, texture is often created by using a palette knife, but anyone who has ever used paint creatively is fully aware that it is impossible to put down an oil colour on canvas, whether with a brush, or any other implement, without giving it personal 'texture'. The exception, of course, comes when the painter forces himself to work in hard-edge style or graphic design style in order to eradicate any personal touch. In textiles, 'hidden' texture is made visible to us by refined weaving techniques, as in damask where pattern is created by the direction of the woven threads, or in satin where shiny surface is contrasted against plain, dull weave. We are often made aware of textures only by contrasts between materials.

The principle of contrast, applicable to any formal values of artistic creation, has a special significance in the case of texture ; in fact, interest and the best relation between the areas of a work of art or a design are created by contrasting texture. Consider contrasting

materials such as stone, bricks, marble, wood, plastics, glass, curtain materials, flooring, and mortar ; and, further, the contrasts of painted areas using shiny oil paint, egg-shell, or emulsion, lacquer and varnish – contrasts, quite apart from the contrasts of colour which can be created by these media, and which spring solely from surface

1960 Pablo Picasso
Homage to Bacchus
lithograph
19¾ × 24¾ in
London Arts Gallery

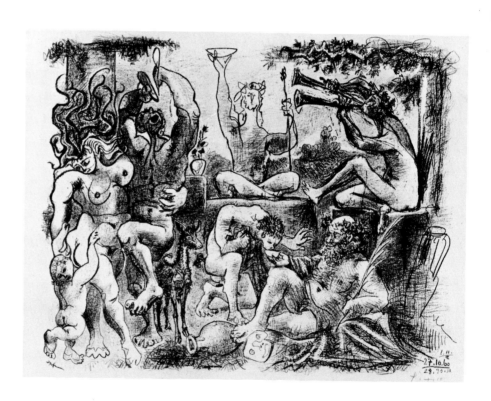

and textural qualities. In an age when the natural texture of any material can be changed or any texture can be created by a manual process, but more often by a chemical or mechanical method, good design training is needed, because textures involving the surface of materials can be critical in creating good *over-all* art and design.

Vision and rhythm

1970 Berenice Sydney
Composition
oil on canvas
48×48 in
private collection

Herbert Ohl and Bernd Meurer
Dormitory 2
project for a students' home
for the Institute of Design
Ulm

1958
Japanese garden
Unesco Building
Paris

The creative idea

The human being distinguishes himself from the animal by creative work. The artist often disregards the immediate aims and applications in the search for good form and new ideas. This creative activity embraces all fields of human life – not only the visual and non-visual arts as such but indeed everything that goes further than the specific functional purpose of an object. Art, in the broadest sense of the word, is any activity that goes further than the basic needs of living. It involves the creation of something special. Naturally, the designed object of functional purpose should have aesthetic value.

The artist feels an urge to create. He cannot force ideas any more than he can create to order. This problem has been well described by Braque, one of the pioneers of modern painting, in his *Cahiers* : 'One must not "think up" a picture. The painter must allow himself to become impregnated by things : he must never interrupt the relationship between them and himself so that they can be free to become a picture whenever they will. Nothing should be forced. I am extremely sensitive to the atmosphere around me, and if I had to try and describe how my pictures happen, I would say that first there is impregnation, then hallucination which turns into an obsession : and in order to free myself from this obsession I *have* to paint.'

1968 Graham Sutherland
Bird form
lithograph
26 × 20 in (66 × 51 cm)
Marlborough Fine Art
London

The human senses

Vision, hearing, smell, taste, and feeling — all these senses play a part in the creation or understanding of a work of art. Furthermore, ideally, good art should involve all, or at least several, of these senses. In experiencing fully a work of art, one not only sees but also hears, feels and may, with some imagination, smell and taste, or simply enjoy the abstract theme, if there is one. Here we must distinguish between figurative and non-figurative art. In figurative art the senses are inspired by the ability of the artist to reproduce facts and to capture moods, in non-figurative work by the sense of invention of the artist or simply by his ability to make the imagination travel, to arouse feelings. These are, however, extremes which only serve to throw some light on the varied approaches and there are many border-line cases. Numerous art movements take their standpoint somewhere between these two extremes, e.g. Impressionism, Expressionism and Surrealism.

c.1930
Francis Picabia
Blue butterflies
gouache
24½ × 18½ in
London Arts Gallery

1969 Joe Tilson
Transparency clip-o-matic eye
screenprint on acetate film
with metallized acetate film
28 × 20 in (71·1 × 50·8 cm)
Marlborough Fine Art
London

1965 Peter Burnhill
Poster
Council of Industrial Design
London

The artist's vision
and the public's perception

Generations of writers and historians have examined and explored
the nature of the artist's vision. However, although the artist, or more
often the designer, has to solve a problem of functional design, the
result cannot always be analysed effectively, for it can never fully be
determined how far he tried to be rational and how far he was carried
away by his ideas, rational or not.

The artist has to examine the perceptive capabilities of the human eye.
A good deal of experience and research is needed to anticipate how
the human eye will react. It can be stated that the human eye will first
of all perceive certain striking characteristics ; but even this statement
has to be taken with some reservation, especially as other factors,
for instance, psychological aspects, can play an important part in
persuading the eye to react.

In fine art we can perhaps examine the question more fully as there
are no functional considerations to be taken into account. The theory
of perception has been explored and described quite often recently,
perhaps because purely non-figurative art lends itself more easily
to an examination of basic concepts. However, it is also much more
difficult to describe than a composition of figurative work. The artist
creates interesting compositions by establishing one or several
focal points which lead the eye into the composition, travelling from
the most prominent element, the introduction, to the next interesting
item. The artist tries to persuade the observer to look at his visual
story completely and in the right sequence.

1965 Peter Burnhill
Poster
Council of Industrial Design
London

1901–04 Auguste Rodin
The Kiss
marble
72½ × 48¼ × 59 in
Tate Gallery
London

1917 Pierre Renoir
Washer-woman
bronze
47½×31¼×50½ in
Tate Gallery
London

The aesthetic sensation

The aesthetic sensation depends on the relationship between the spectator and the work of art or design. Sculpture is ideally suited to illustrate an ever-changing relationship because it is three-dimensional. Here the spectator need not content himself with a flat, frontal view, but can experience continuously new visual 'sensations' by walking around the sculpture, thus exhausting all possible view points. A front view will perhaps give a purely aesthetic experience of the over-all conception of the *œuvre*, which does not differ much from looking at a two-dimensional work such as a painting or a flat relief. Walking around a piece of sculpture is a good approach to capturing the feeling of movement and often enables us to experience this movement almost physically, as well as to explore the spiritual attitude, *l'esprit* of the work. Movement becomes revelation. Again, in a work of art which is taken from life, as for example in the *Washer-woman* by Renoir of 1917, where the woman is entirely absorbed in her work, feeling herself entirely unobserved, the method of 'looking-over-the-shoulder' could well serve as the introduction to the sculpture, before we look at this statue from the front or *en profile.* In Rodin's *Kiss* of 1901–04, the movement of the two figures leads the eye, without any effort, around the composition. The eye follows, instinctively, this movement which springs from profound emotion and fulfilment in union. Michelangelo's sculpture, again, can perhaps best be studied by looking at it in a sequence identical to that which Michelangelo employed in chiselling the work, namely from the foundation to the top, as his creation was born out of the marble block. The eye will travel from the foundation of the marble with its

1969 Lynn Chadwick
Maquette II for Elektra
bronze
height 31 in (79 cm)
Marlborough Fine Art
London

rough *non finiti* parts, to those parts smoothed to a high finish, a technique which incidentally already forecasts the beginnings of Mannerism. In proceeding in this way, the spectator will have an opportunity to familiarize himself a little better with the imagination and vision of the artist and to re-experience his procedure of creating a work of art. Another example : the frontal view of a building, seen from a distance, makes the building appear as a part of the town environment or the landscape. By contrast, a walk around the building, a kind of physical investigation by 'feeling' with the eyes, can become an experience of space. A further possibility would involve examining a building and its surroundings from above, from a plane, or from the top of a tower. Both physical nearness and physical distance can contribute to no small extent towards the right aesthetic experience of a work of art or design. The question as to what are the most effective means and conditions for a fully enjoyable aesthetic sensation remains for the individual to decide, according to his temperament.

1966 Gerd Richter
Emma – nude on staircase
oil
200×130 cm
Collection Peter Ludwig

8th–9th centuries,
with later additions
Mosque
Cordoba, Spain

Articulate and inarticulate form

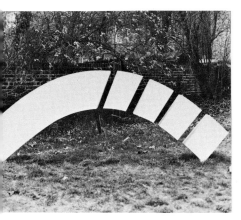

Contrary to common belief, in art and design it is not always necessary to make everything explicit by using elements that can be perceived and analysed immediately. Not everyone realizes that the eye and indeed the imagination frequently supplement and compensate for missing elements in a composition. As a result of this, the observer assumes that the missing element is in fact present. The eye of the onlooker also sometimes creates rhythm where it does not exist and often continues such rhythmical arrangements and compositions to the extent unconsciously desired. The eye sees and complements the missing parts quite easily, often without being detected by the conscious mind. We all know that a truly searching mind and time are needed to discover such missing parts. The human eye will continue to see horizontal and vertical lines and elements, even when these are not completely and consequently carried through, e.g. in a work of architecture.

There are articulate and inarticulate form elements hidden in the structure of a work of art and design. Later we will deal with the articulate or conscious structure of things. Let us consider for a moment the inarticulate or unconscious form elements. It would be interesting to examine the perception process by which we can create or enjoy the hidden structure of a work of art. But is this possible ? Fortunately, only to a certain extent. To analyse non-figurative art, we must almost psychoanalyse – as the subject matter is often missing. Inarticulate form is inclined to escape a logical analysis more easily than distinct or articulate form. Inarticulate

1472–94 Niklas Esler and Son
Stadtkirche St Georg
Dinkelbühl

begun 1903
Antonio Gaudì
La sagrada familia
Barcelona

form elements have been compared with some of the scale-free nuances in music, which the composer uses to make his work more lively, more expressive. They may also be called the artist's intimate style by which his work, and often forgeries, can be traced – his personal 'calligraphy' as it were.

All these conscious and unconscious elements of form play an important part in the process of artistic creation. In particular, but not exclusively, in abstract art, form elements such as point, line, area, body and volume, surface, texture and structure, and colour provide an essential framework and often the essence itself. Certainly, in non-figurative art, inarticulate or unconscious form elements develop fully, and thus come to their full *Entfaltung*, their full growth. The soul and hand of the artist is uncovered and displayed. Non-figurative work is the personal handwriting of the artist. This latest development of art which, as shown in other chapters, existed to some extent in all periods, is important for the designer of today, who often relies no longer on figurative, ornamental work to decorate his products, but on form that is aesthetically good, on structure that has precise and basic quality in its own right.

Rhythm

Rhythm is created when we see or arrange objects in isolation or in relation, when we see things as a whole or in detail. The eye movements of the observer have to be calculated in advance by the designer, the artist, the architect. Just as a good poster should have an 'eye-catcher', the same applies to product design, and certainly to architecture. In product design this 'eye-catcher' will be related to function : e.g. how to design an electric iron, a wireless-set, a television set, a tape-recorder, a washing machine, in a way that the button, that has to be pressed to operate the product, can be found easily ; how to design a product that will be spontaneously handled in the right way, even by the amateur.

The pictorial and symbolic properties of lines, planes and solids have to be psychologically used by the designer. Size or rather proportional or relative size is important. A certain object is expected to have a certain size, and has to be designed accordingly ; unless one wants to create a shock — as is often useful in publicity work, where objects are greatly enlarged or reduced in size to create attention. In order to accord with the eye movements in perception, it is necessary, amongst other things, to create in the design a relationship that will give the intended aesthetic sensation : direction, sequence and rhythm, interval, separation, tension, anticipation, surprise and revelation, harmony and contrast and graduation. The eye of the observer must be led by the artist. To achieve this, the basic arrangement of a design project, the correct planning of town and landscape and the composition of a painting, must be considered and conceived in

Rhine bridge
near Emmerich

Rhine Bridge
Duisburg-Rheinhausen

advance by the artist and designer. Often the properties of textures, the correct conception of space, depth, volume, the right measure of active and passive elements in the design or work of art assist in this, provided they are properly exploited.

Although no special gift is needed to feel rhythm, space, depth, and volume, it may help to analyse these aspects by looking at the work of those who are actively involved in creating the environment, the shape of products and the imagery of the fine arts. Architecture, especially, which lays some claim to being the mother art – on which all other arts should ideally be based or to which they should be related – enables us to see, feel, and experience rhythm and space directly. Although the nature of architecture is functional, space has to be arranged to satisfy emotionally as well as functionally. A knowledge of architectural style should, therefore, be combined with the aesthetic outlook which sees in architecture the revelation of beautifully composed space with a satisfying relationship which is sometimes quite obvious, sometimes hidden, or invisible, or sometimes waiting to be discovered – full of force and tension.

The architecture of the past can teach us a great deal about these aspects but perhaps even more does modern architecture. Contemporary planning does not want to be hindered by classical orders and prescribed composition but experiments freely with space and rhythm in composing units, blocks and areas of various form and size, but always to meet the basic needs of modern living and to be

Prater Stadium
Vienna

aesthetically satisfactory. In good architecture, materials for building
are considered elements to express, as far as possible, functional
requirements and aesthetic principles. Although architecture exists
to provide shelter, in any civilized society it will mean more: a
composition for living, an art form in its own right.

Telephone exchange
Cologne

New Philharmonic Hall
Berlin
(Herbert von Karajan conducting)

1966 Lynn Chadwick
Moon Series F
lithograph
19¾ × 25⅝ in
(50·2 × 65·1 cm)
Marlborough Fine Art
London

The eternal cycle

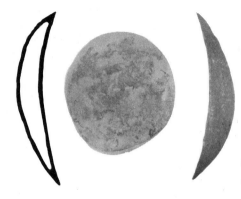

In discussing rhythm in art, a comparison of art with the rhythm to be found in human life is quite revealing. Examining this aspect more closely, it can be noticed that human life is based on an eternal rhythm of day and night, in tune with the endless cycle of the seasons. Of course, this is taken for granted and hardly even noticed by urban man. But primitive societies whose whole way of life and standard of living still depend directly on the success of the sowing and harvest, on whether there is rain or drought, celebrate the cycle of seasons in extensive joyful ceremonies of thanksgiving, but they also pray for and celebrate the return of the sun and the coming of the rain. This is very consciously and profoundly expressed in their art.

Although the laws of nature and nature itself may play a great part in inspiring art and design, the artist or designer is usually not content with this; nor does he rely too much on history and established systems of order and rhythm. He will always attempt to create fascinating new rhythms in which functional and aesthetic requirements are given necessary consideration. To create rhythm we need more than one element of form. The degree of harmony obtainable will depend on the properties of these elements. Two identical elements will create harmony; two opposing elements will create contrast. Basically, symmetry is considered to radiate or to express harmony and tranquillity, while asymmetry brings about contrast, disturbance, strong emotions. Harmony or contrast can be created by endless variations of form and colour.

1966 David Holmes
Poster for Gas Council
Council of Industrial Design
London

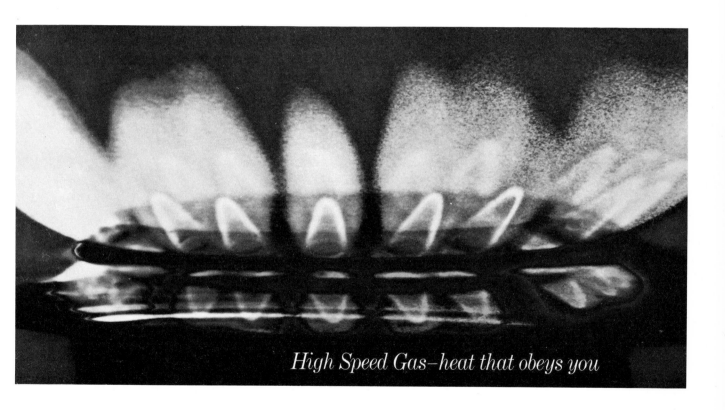

High Speed Gas—heat that obeys you

W. Zobel
Administration Offices
Nordhorn near Bentheim

While the seasons demonstrate an almost strictly regular rhythm, which, if upset, disturbs human life and brings disasters such as famine and floods, in art, more often than not, irregular rhythm can be found. Rhythm in art is the grouping of form elements : the arrangement of basic units, for example in architecture, in painting, in sculpture and in industrial design. It can also be the accumulation and multiple use of one kind of material, resulting in a certain rhythmical movement that is not purely decorative. This kind of rhythmical grouping, movement or emphasis can be achieved by stressing a typical characteristic, or by stressing volume, or by combinations, i.e. tall against small, long against short, thick against thin. In finding rhythmical stress, the diverse domains of art and design do not basically differ from the fields of the non-visual arts. In fact, it is quite immaterial whether distinguishable values of rhythm are created by the sequence of steps in dancing, syllables in speaking, staccato notes in music or by form and colour in the visual arts.

Regular rhythm is produced by repeating identical or related intervals or shades, a gradation that could be equally applied to fields which deal with phonetic or visual values of volume. *Irregular rhythm* is produced by the repetition of dissimilar, opposing and varied elements of accentuation. A pure and simple or accidental variety of elements does not necessarily produce harmony or rhythm, although it can, as happened in some of Arp's work which he purposely 'arranged according to the laws of chance'. True rhythm embraces skilful adjustment and arrangement and, last but not least, requires masterly

Philip Thompson
Brochure for Rotaflex

1964 Josef Küpper
House of houses
project
consisting of 25 stories of
individual houses

1958 Hans Arp
High-relief
bronze
Unesco Building
Paris

repetition of such elements in order to produce a true *œuvre*. Bach dealt with the problem in *The Art of the Fugue*, and it is surely not without reason that generations of artists have attempted to capture the rhythm of music in works of visual art.

1965 Horst-Peter Dollinger
Tower Hotel
Essen

1970 Joe Tilson
Ziggurat
wood and stainless steel
7×7×7 in (17·8×17·8×17·8 cm)
Marlborough Graphics
London

Looking at art

Gate at Hampton Court
photographed by the author

1960–63 Iginio Balderi
Columns
height 230 cm
private collection

Retour à la nature?

No one can give an adequate verbal explanation of an optical or mechanical object. The Chinese proverb 'A picture is worth a thousand words' still holds true in our century. The written word helps to describe what we see, think, hear, feel, smell. But words have to be used in a constructive way because an oversimplified introduction to art can do more harm than good. A way must be found of coming to understand a work of art by the use of all the human faculties. In positive terms: a right balance between original expression and thought and knowledge of aesthetic and historical principles is best for the creative artist and the observer of art.

The modern artist and designer cannot entirely isolate himself from convention. He cannot suddenly become say neo-prehistoric, just by deciding to do so. He cannot, dwelling in cities, practise Rousseau's *Retour à la nature,* because he is a citizen of today serving and being guided by his environment. There is a lot of truth in the advice given from time to time by artists, e.g. Courbet, Toulouse-Lautrec, Picasso, to close all museums for some time to allow the artist to find his own style, and not to be influenced too much by the past. Obviously, however, some historical information and theory of art and design are indispensable.

Rock outcrops in the
Teuteburg Forest
originally a centre of
prehistoric cults

Art and nature

Generally speaking art is either transformed nature (naturalistic, figurative art) or abstracted nature (abstract, non-figurative art); seldom is it unrelated to nature, even in a distant way. Of course, there are artists who like nature but not its substitute, nature in art, as, for instance, Arp: 'I love nature but not its substitute'. Mondrian is known to have turned his back on nature, and especially on the colour of nature, green. When invited to the houses of friends, he refused to look at the garden. This does not mean that the artist did not like nature as such. He just did not want nature to hinder him from finding a visual language of his own. The struggle of the artist in depicting nature or being inspired by nature has been recorded throughout the history of mankind, and the influence of nature on all fields of art – Western and Oriental – is well known.

Artists of all periods have abstracted from nature. In ancient Egypt the lotus plant served as a prototype for the development of form in capitals. Almost every period finds in nature a different prototype for the decoration of capitals. A regularized form of the acanthus, a free-growing plant, appears in the Corinthian order of Greek and Roman architecture. The structure of a tree and its use in primitive building inspired Oriental and Classical art alike in the visual and structural conception of temples and secular buildings, side by side with pure geometric forms, as in the pyramids.

In painting and sculpture the period which best represents the influence of nature on art is the Renaissance, with its search for a

1889 Vincent van Gogh
View of Arles
oil on canvas
72×92 cm
Bayerische Staatsgemäldesammlungen
Munich

1970 Erich Reusch
Electrostatic objects
plexiglass, pigment, static
electricity
each object 200 × 100 × 40 cm
private collection

happy blend of nature and abstraction in contrast to the stylized art of the Byzantine and medieval periods. The difficulties stemming from attempts to depict nature are perhaps best illustrated by a remark of Constable who is well known for his contribution to landscape painting : 'The art of seeing nature is a thing almost as much to be acquired as the art of reading the hieroglyphs.'

Contemporary graphic and industrial design definitely tend towards a more abstract interpretation of nature simply for reasons dictated by the medium, by the speed of production, and, most of all, by functional considerations, such as legibility and comfort. The graphic artist designing a poster simplifies or symbolizes nature rather than depicting nature itself in order that he might attract the attention of the public, who pass his poster in a hurry. Furniture throughout the ages demanded organic ornament, springing from the nature of the material and its structure. This compelled the designer to abstract from nature for purposes of decoration and ornament. Revivals as in William Morris's Arts and Crafts movement or in Art Nouveau, were followed, however, by modern art, architecture and design in which function and proportions displaced the importance of ornament derived from nature. The artist of the contemporary period definitely feels this influence. Picasso on being asked about his attitude towards nature stated : 'They always talk of naturalism as being the opposite to modern painting. I would be interested to know whether anyone has ever seen a natural work of art. Nature and art are two entirely different things. Thus they can never be identical.'

The object

In all periods artists embody different attitudes towards their subject matter. Even the simplest of everyday objects can be made rich in expression under creative hands. Sometimes the artist gives them a second, perhaps surrealistic, symbolic or abstract nature. The most natural inspiration will come from the simple and basic forces and phenomena which nature displays : sea, sky, sun, moon, stone.

Abstract ideas and notions are much more difficult to express in visual terms, for instance, beauty, peace, colour, duration, heat. The artist will have to rely very much on his own imagination and the association given to these abstract ideas by the public he is approaching. A physical activity is much more difficult to translate into art than a simple still life. Artists of our time have developed action painting, which does not show an object or a person in action, but the traces of action itself. To depict a musical instrument or people making music is one thing ; the abstract interpretation of music as such or the sensation caused by music another. To depict a car does not necessarily translate the sensation of speed. In most cases the artist will, therefore, find a compromise between association and abstraction. It is by no means sufficient to reflect nature in the manner of the reflection in a mirror in order to create art. The mystical spell of art is an essential part of the task. A work of art need not necessarily be beautiful, but it must be hypnotic in such a way that the observer does not remain indifferent.

Form

Form is a more general term than *shape.* While shape is more often
applied in the practical sense, the term form can be used also in the
philosophical, abstract-symbolic or romantic sense. While shape is
mostly used for two-dimensional work, form is mainly used to
describe the third dimension in art and design. Often these two terms
overlap. Another definition of form is the shape given to an object by
the designer. Although there is absolute form in the abstract sense,
those who are looking for the visual sensation will notice that the
actual appearance of form can vary substantially through environment,
climatic conditions or through factors of time : the hour of the day or
the season of the year. In visual terms it can be assumed that form is
determined by the space it occupies, in other words, by the way it is
positioned. Form should be, first of all, pleasing to the eye, while at
the same time fulfilling necessary, functional considerations.

To achieve good form has been the preoccupation of artists and
designers as long as humanity has existed. Frequently, the artists have
purposely experimented with very simple forms in order to find a new
visual language, as did Braque and Picasso in the years 1910–11
when they were involved in establishing the principles of Cubism.
But this search for simplicity of form is by no means confined to the
pioneers of modern art and design. In all periods and schools a new
style was found by abolishing the old. In most cases a richer or more
elaborate style was replaced by a new simple language or form. This
in its turn became more elaborate while in fashion, and was then
replaced by a new style, with its own simple form. Egyptian, Classical

1923 Rudolf Belling
Sculpture 23
Galerie Wolfgang Ketterer
Munich

1950 Henry Moore
Helmet
Cecil Higgins Museum
Bedford

1967 Ben Nicholson
Torcello I
etching
13¾×18⅛ in
(35×38·5 cm)
Marlborough Fine Art
London

Greek and Roman art, and Gothic art began as basically simple forms that were then elaborated, becoming richer and richer. Gothic form, having reigned for some three or four centuries throughout the art world of Europe, gave way to a Renaissance of Classical Roman form in the fifteenth century. After the richness and volume of Baroque art had developed into the more precise and detailed form of Rococo ornament, again a revival took place. This, the mid-eighteenth century movement called neo-Classicism, preferred once more Classical form and its Renaissance interpretation.

The many art movements of the nineteenth and twentieth centuries all had as their basic aim the search for new form. Frequently, a new form was found by anti-art, by protesting against the past. A consideration of this process may help us to understand more recent experiments in form by the modern movement. They explain the serious purpose of the artist and designer in striving for new form, often paying scant regard to the reaction of the general public or of the critics. Those who achieved the best results in this periodic searching for new form are now often the established leaders of art movements. Of today's experiments, no doubt, only the best will remain to recall the visual language of form of our time.

1969 Pierre Alechinsky
Dormeur debout
acrylic on canvas
30 × 39 in
London Arts Gallery

Distortion is, strictly speaking, anything that does not copy or imitate wholly the 'photographic' appearance of an object. Naturally, the human eye has learned to adjust itself to a certain extent, but every individual will reach a point when he will find distortion intolerable, when it is incomprehensible to the intellect. Furthermore, every civilization will have a different 'distortion-barrier'. This might well be in Western art, perhaps, the degree of distortion in Post-impressionism, while members of Eastern or African civilizations may not consider anything distorted except completely non-figurative work and even then they might find a symbolic meaning in it. In fact, the members of primitive societies will sometimes find considerable trouble in sorting out the outlines in photographs, getting confused by the richness and variety of different tone values. In contrast, they will have no trouble at all in reading a visual meaning into the abstraction or distortion in a simple line drawing, as they are accustomed to look out for the essential, the interesting. This is similar to the visual apprehension of a child, who observes the fascinating details, and ignores cheerfully the correct proportions of individual objects or of the composition as a whole.

Distortion is often demanded subconsciously by the creative mind, which basically makes the decision to shape and compose in a certain way. Often the artist wakes up from his visual dreamland quite surprised to find that the public cannot appreciate certain forms,

Last supper
The Black Church
Göreme Nevşehir
Turkey

Jan Mostaert
The Holy Family at Table
oak panel 37 × 24 cm
Wallraf-Richartz-Museum
Cologne

arrangements or structures. He is astonished to notice that some people understand and others fail to do so, whilst still others may read a different meaning into the distorted subject, far beyond the artist's intention.

The public of today does not find Oriental or Byzantine or Russian art distorted beyond a tolerable degree, nor the works of Gothic art or of 'modern' artists such as Toulouse-Lautrec or Van Gogh. Today, we completely forget that much Oriental art was discovered and fully exploited hardly a century ago in the West. In architecture the decisive change to freely composed and distorted forms took place only after the collapse of eclectic styles, and was brought about by those whom we consider the pioneers of modern art and architecture. This way of thinking begins with Art Nouveau which freely distorts Celtic form and the plant ornament. An example of distortion of quite a different kind is found in the work of Mondrian, who very much admired Romanesque architecture for its simplicity and universality of form.

In Egyptian or early Greek art proportions were always idealized, giving to the human body proportions which are anatomically impossible. The realistic approach was introduced by the Romans who did not want to idealize but to record minutely their victories and to depict features of their Caesars. It is well known that the Romans managed to introduce their Graeco-Roman style into all the occupied territories, but never into Egypt, which had had for too long a tradition of symbolic abstraction or distortion.

Considerable distortion appears in the works of Mannerists such as Parmigianino in his elegant *Madonna del Collo Lungo*, very shortly after the high period of the Renaissance, and even in the work of Michelangelo which forecasts the style of Baroque. It appears equally in the long-necked creations of the eighteenth-century school of English portraiture as in the works of Gainsborough. We do not really mind this degree of distortion, in fact we appear to like it, because it is elegant.

c.1535
Francesco Parmigianino
Madonna del Collo Lungo
Uffizi
Florence

c.1750
Thomas Gainsborough
Mr and Mrs Andrews
detail
National Gallery
London

Movement and motion

Movement is the natural or mechanical motion of an object. Explored by the artist or designer, either by direct means as in kinetic art, or by perspective and *trompe-l'œil* as in conventional painting, it leads the eye in a certain direction. Movement is form that 'pulls' strongly. As an abstract art term, it is closely related to growth. Without movement, a work of art is static and may be boring to look at for a long time. Movement adds interest. Movement is necessary to give impact to a work of art or design. Works that are too passive in conception have little effect on the onlooker. Our age is the age of movement and it is not without reason that art has followed this trend.

Let us see how movement occurs in a work of art or design. A composition usually consists of several focal points or even a single focal point towards which all the other elements are visually directed or to which they give visual support. There seems to be a quiet or harmonious co-existence between static elements and swinging elements. The onlooker passes over the different planes or concentration of elements of a composition, one after the other, because his eye is simply not capable of taking in everything at once.

The sequence of such observation cannot always be anticipated : people sometimes look at books from back to front, glancing at the illustrations, and not, as the author had intended, from front to back. The artist who wants the attention of the public would do well to keep in mind that the human being is an animal who is inclined to be

Raphael
(1483–1520)
Madonna della sedia
Pitti Palace
Florence

lazy, who basically only works when there is a direct need, be it of a financial or moral nature. He will therefore only look at an object properly when a real visual interest has been aroused.

Movement, in a work of fine art and design, is determined by active and passive elements which contrast with or complement one another. Modern art tries to do away with the conventional belief that movement is restricted to the work of musicians, actors and dancers. The artists of our age question whether the expression of movement should be limited to theatre and dance. In our mechanical age the expression of movement in art should not be restricted to the portrayal of the physical properties and limitations of the human or animal body. Today the mechanical motion of cars, aircraft and spaceships are totally accepted and there is no reason why they cannot provide an inspiration for art forms. In fact humanity has always tried to create or record movement by a variety of devices, and the artist has always tried to depict the latest devices. The invention of the wheel is in itself the very symbol of motion; the sun dial was invented to record the movement of the sun; later, refined clockwork mechanisms moved precisely and accurately. The simple forerunner of the cinema and slow-motion camera, the latest screen techniques creating three-dimensional effects, and indeed the manifold application and creative use of light and colour, are all inventions of humanity to create movement or the illusion of it by mechanical means.

1912 Giacomo Balla
Child running on a balcony
Galleria d'Arte Moderna
Milan

166

In depicting movement, the artist is expressing his comment about time, change and sequence. Expressed in abstract terms, he is trying to recall movement as such, which means not something that one can trace, but something that moves in its own right and is not necessarily related to figurative, pictorial objectivity. In this, he is on the same lines as modern science which has demonstrated that human or any other form of existence is never static but always follows the principles of change and motion. These activities embrace a wide range of different movements, from the growing of a plant to travelling at speed. The painter or sculptor of movement not only captures the element of time, but establishes a value that does not depend upon actual motion but is independent of it.

The art of our century has set out to record motion, in visual terms, as never captured before. Microscopic observations and slow motion pictures allow us to see the cells actually grow in animal and human life itself, and space-flight extends our scale to enable us to see the movements of whole continents, the atmosphere and even the cosmos. The artist tries to express in a new visual language that which we could always observe, but which today we can see and inspect so much more easily. The water-drop, the snow crystal, a cloud of steam – all these have been depicted by painters for centuries, but only recently as art elements in their own right. Painters such as Turner and Constable were very sensitive to the pattern created by moving clouds. Looking back to the fantastic efforts of Baroque art to create movement with truly theatrical refinement, we notice that

1913 Giacomo Balla
Automobile in motion
Galleria d'Arte Moderna
Milan

basically nothing has changed. Our dynamic age merely lends itself
more easily to the realization of the centuries-old dreams of artists,
who have always been searching for new means of expressing
movement and motion.

Speed in art

Ever since the days of Baroque the element of speed in art has become more pronounced. The swinging rhythm of the Baroque line is perhaps the most dominant characteristic of the seventeenth century, when the revived Classical idealism of Renaissance art gave way to a more cheerful and life-enhancing approach. It is not without reason that this progression from Classical to Baroque art has made some art theorists refer to late Greek art as already having Baroque properties of speed, and this is indeed a logical development. In fact the whole period of art history in terms of styles has sometimes been simplified to an ever-changing manifestation of Classical and Baroque form, but this makes too many demands on the more concise meaning of the term Baroque.

Indeed just as Baroque art and architecture, the sculptures of Bernini, the châteaux of Hildebrandt, and the paintings of Rubens have little in common with the preceding Renaissance style, so the full-blooded and lively Romanticism of the nineteenth century has little in common with the early, austere neo-Classicism of the preceding age. Romanticism certainly expresses speed to an extent unknown hitherto and therefore demonstrates a true revolution of visual attitude. This is revealed in the works of Géricault, for example, which are alive and which vividly demonstrate the element of speed and are very modern in feeling, although still relying on figurative subject matter.

During the last decades of the nineteenth century neo-Baroque and especially Art Nouveau clearly broke away in temperament from the Classical attitude. The prototype of Art Nouveau, the swinging

1966 John Nixon
photo by Louis Klementaski
Poster for British Rail Inter-City
Council of Industrial Design
London

and 'stylized in motion' plant element, replaced the dried out historicism and eclecticism of the past and showed the way which modern styles depicting speed were to take in the twentieth century. Munch and Van Gogh in their pioneer work in the direction of Expressionism; the Fauves, the 'wild beasts' of rough, rapid and provoking colour; Kandinsky, in his increasingly abstract and in the end completely non-figurative painting, all show most clearly the element of speed. The Futurists, proclaiming in a Manifesto in 1911, the aesthetic superiority of a fast car over a work of Classical Greek sculpture, are perhaps those who most inspire the present generation. Not so much by their works but by their indirect guidance, they encourage today's artists who practise speed in art in the most direct way, in action painting, where the vehicle itself is performing the action of speed, producing a painting that carries this property of speed as the dominating element.

Some speed architecture and speed sculpture does not simply suggest the capacity of speed by three-dimensional illusion, but creates it through the rotations of a motor, in forms of kinetic art which are an intermarriage of sculptured form, light and speed. A comparison of the modern but classical art of Rodin and the purely experimental and non-figurative work of Moholy-Nagy is revealing in this respect.

Speed through colour motion in Op and Pop art is another aspect of the revolution, as is poster or television design to which some fine art of today owes a great deal of inspiration.

1967 Laura Grisi
Model car racing
environment with 4 different
objects on 16 polished steel plates
Galerie Klaus Lüpke
Frankfurt/Main

Creating tension

Tension can be translated into visual terms in many different ways. It is certainly a property of the kind of art which is truly overpowering and exciting, and can create a spell either in purely visual terms or in psychological or philosophical terms. Tension is an element that is introduced spontaneously by the artist and can seldom be planned and calculated in advance, except perhaps in more abstract non-figurative or concrete art. The artist, of course, knows that the human being can be persuaded by an appeal to his sentiments. He is also appealing, however, to human reactions that cannot be foreseen, but are in fact decided from moment to moment, and he knows that very little in human reaction is strictly logical and that these moments of logic are rare and short-lived. Equally short-lived are visual works that express an experience in such a superficial way. Pictures of lust or cold beauty, for example, may create the same kind of mild visual tension as a pin-up photograph or a cartoon. Such works will give visual pleasure that is as short-lasting as the corresponding physical experience. Tension expressing visual idealism or doctrinaire feeling may prove to be quite out of tune with today's philosophy and way of thinking, and thus will make no impact on the younger generation.

Modern art embodies the tensions of modern life. The visual interpretation of tension changes, of course, with the taste of the time. Van Gogh's work, embodying his wavy lines of tension, was at first violently rejected by the general public of his day which was not accustomed to such expressions. The next generation was to swing, a few decades later, to complete admiration.

A. Guzman
Tensione 125
marble
140×80 cm
Biennale Internazionale
di Scultura, Carrara
Foto Cav. I. Bessi

In non-figurative work the element of tension is used successfully, perhaps more often than we realize. It tends to be 'disguised' in the applied arts and in design. We apparently do not mind abstract visual language in this area, and are prepared to overlook the fact that the abstract shapes in design were often inspired by the abstract works of corresponding movements in the fine arts. Perhaps very simple examples can illustrate the abstract quality of the element 'tension' in a work of art or design. Tension can be caused by two or more elements, with one in a certain relationship to the other(s), e.g. contrasts of position, size, volume, colour, pattern, texture, surface, or material. Tension is the 'pulling' of matter or of elements either in a painting or in a three-dimensional work. Bad proportions may cause quite unwanted tension ; where, for example, balance is sought in the composition by the artist or designer, tension must not be uneven. Tension can be increased by complementary shapes and it can be created by the movement of design elements in opposing directions, though here, perhaps, tension is subsidiary to movement.

Thomas Gainsborough
(1727–88)
Study of trees
$5\frac{9}{16} \times 7\frac{1}{2}$ in
(14·1×19 cm)
British Museum
London

Edouard Manet
(1832–83)
Monsieur Armand on horseback
Galleria d'Arte Moderna
Milan

The physique of art and design

The artist and designer can represent an object by using material of a totally different nature to that employed in the original. The material in the hands of the artist and designer achieves a life of its own, ranging from the naturalistic to the symbolic, abstract, and non-figurative. The material is a partner, sharing the creative process with the artist and designer. It is a process of giving and taking. The creative activity is a sequence of experiments concerned with problems of expression and form in a work of art. The visualizing in the artist's mind takes place long before he thinks about the physique, the material needed to create the work. However, visual creation can sometimes work the other way round, starting from experiments with the material itself, rather like a composer who receives inspiration from trying out an instrument. Even visual roughs done without any artistic or creative intention, inspired simply by a pattern or ink-blob, may lead to the definitive conception of a design, a painting, a work of sculpture or architecture.

The surface of a wall may have inspired the cave-man to create his crude paintings. Michelangelo has been quoted as saying that his sculptures were inspired by the material. Certainly stone or marble will hint positively at possible shapes, will suggest form itself and the simplification of form that the sculptor had originally in mind. The limitations of a block of marble have often obliged the artist to think again — to look at his work with a fresh eye. In this, Michelangelo does not differ too much from Moore who states that some of his work is inspired by the unintended 'works' of nature. Properties and

Andrea del Verrocchio
(1435–88)
Florentine
Lorenzo de' Medici
terracotta
Samuel H. Kress Collection
National Gallery of Art
Washington

principles underlying the material used, in any creative activity, will introduce new, interesting, often revealing features into a work of art or design, provided of course the artist is alive to them, can see or feel them, and explore them fully and creatively. The technique by which the physique of a work of art or design is created is usually very personal to and characteristic of a particular artist; it is indeed his imprint on an idea, thus conceived and visualized. The way in which the work is given form and expression, the way in which idea and execution merge into each other in a work, varies endlessly from artist to artist, from period to period. Some artists have a surfeit of ideas which they have to sort out before it is at all possible to put them into material terms; they strive to leave out all that is unnecessary in order to find the essential. Others have to work hard to keep their creative power going, finding that their first idea was good but is in need of a great deal of development to justify it as a work of art. Some take little preparation and paint *alla prima*, that is, directly onto the canvas without any previous sketches or painting. Having only a vague idea in their mind, they paint in a mad rush, to achieve all or nothing. Others need hours and hours of preparation, numerous sketches, weeks of study and research, only to put everything aside to create the actual work of art in the shortest time possible, in isolation with material and technique.

Furthermore, there are certain principles and properties of the material itself which the artist has to observe whether he is revolutionary or conventional in his approach. Most modern art was created not only

Mino da Fiesole
(1429–84)
Florentine
Astorgio Manfredi
marble
Widener Collection
National Gallery of Art
Washington

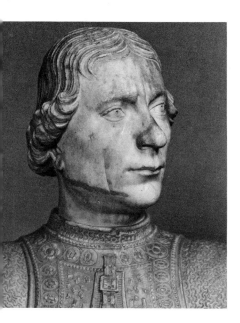

by anti-art in the spiritual sense, but also in the material sense, that is by applying forms and material contrary to conventional usage. Being inventive, these anti-art artists created, in most cases, lively, new, material principles both in fine art and design. Examples of this are numerous : the experiments of synthetic Cubism which involved the application of actual materials to the canvas as part of the composition, the Dadaists and Surrealists who created new rhythms and aesthetic principles, or the designers who departed from traditional craftsmanship to plan for machine-production in industrial design. By experimenting endlessly, these *avant-garde* artists established not only new creative possibilities for new materials, but in so doing founded an entirely new conception of art and design form.

It would be wrong to consider materials as merely physical things, merely necessities to help the artist, and well below the dignity and indeed the interest of the art critic. This would imply refusal to recognize that materials are an integral part of the artist's and designer's venture, the very foundation on which his work can grow. Anyone seeing an artist handling with great care and involvement the material, the physical basis of his work, will understand how intimate the contact between artist and material can be, whether in fine or functional art. Basically there is no difference between handling a bulk of clay in free experimental art or in testing the texture of a new material in functional design and architecture. Fortunately, more and more interest is shown by an inquiring public in the nature of materials. This, to no small extent, is due to the fact that modern

Antonio Rossellino
(1427–78)
Florentine
The young Saint John the Baptist
marble
Kress Collection
National Gallery of Art
Washington

1967 Pietro Cascella
Detail of sculpture
marble
Galleria Arte Borgogna
Milan
Foto Cav. I. Bessi
Carrara

painting often reveals the qualities and properties of the material itself, in both figurative and non-figurative art. It is also due to the gradual disappearance of ornamentation and decoration in contemporary architecture and design, which lays bare the properties of the materials employed.

Materials are for the artist or the designer akin to the instrument for the musician. The artist need not be involved in making the pigment or getting a block of marble, just as a musician does not have to make his own instrument – but a thorough knowledge of materials helps the artist to create and to explore the inherent possibilities and opportunities. Considered in this strict sense, materials as such are not really part of the aesthetic value of a work of art or design. The artist's sensitivity towards materials and instruments is more likely to be based on an urge to apply them with greater virtuosity. Indeed, it has been said that materials or instruments can become part of the artist, meaning that he gets so accustomed to them, that he handles them as if they were part of himself. This can be compared to a horseman who knows his horse so well, that he senses all his reactions in advance. Just as the rider does not need to be concerned with breeding horses or the driver with manufacturing cars, the artist does not need to be involved in producing the materials he uses for his art. But all are *connoisseurs* in selecting the best to make their activity a success – the artist with his painting or sculpture as much as the horseman or racing-car driver who is battling to win.

Criticism and philosophy

The almost surrealistic experience
of water cut by the keel of
a fast motor boat
photographed by the author

1781 Johann Heinrich Füssli
Nightmare
oil on canvas
75·5×64 cm
Freies Deutsches Hochstift
Frankfurter Goethemuseum
Frankfurt/Main

Phenomenon and phantom

While a scientific phenomenon proper can be observed and analysed, the aesthetic phenomenon of art can only be experienced with the senses. Not without reason the term phenomenon is applied in a more general way to the extraordinary, the remarkable, the out-of-the-common. Seen from this point of view, we could, of course, classify outstanding art as phenomenal, a surrealistic experience, lifting human nature into a 'higher sphere' – a romantic term for which a more up-to-date replacement cannot easily be found. *Phenomenalism* is a theory of Kant (1724–1804) which takes into account only the appearance of things (*Erscheinungen*) not their overall character (*Wesen*) and the meanings that lie behind them. However, Hegel (1770–1831) in his *Phenomenology of Spirit* of 1807 searches for the inner experience and he is therefore often quoted by those who see in art and design something more than vehicles to communicate facts and realistic features. 'Being' and 'thinking' are for Hegel identical, and this conception can help us to realize that a work of art and design and the experience caused by it are in fact *one*. They cannot be separated from each other even though we might talk about them as if they were separate. Hegel writes that the laws of nature, the history and evolution of mankind, art and religion and the self-examination and self analyses of the human mind are all in fact contributing towards the spiritual nature of the universe, and this theory could be easily applied to any creative process, be it visual or non-visual. Art and all the underlying factors which go towards its creation are inseparable.

1900 Edward Reginal Frampton
The childhood of Neptune
oil on canvas
117×167 cm
Galleria del Levante
Milan

1967 Erich Reusch
Plastik
600×240 cm
private collection

The modern approach to art and design is linked to nineteenth-century theories of philosophy that have only been put into practice in our century. Today, art is no longer considered as an exclusively rational exercise or a tiresome process of imitation and illusion to satisfy the intellect alone. Hegel definitely finds a workable foundation for a philosophy of art that is built upon ideas and an all-embracing perception, in which the sympathy towards a work of art or music is just as important as the purely rational engagement. Today it is quite obvious that the non-rational is the inspiration for the rational, which is the inspiration translated into physical terms. Modern psychology believes that there are few things the human mind plans logically and carries out logically. The non-rational laws of the co-incident, so easily accepted by some non-European civilizations, have come back into Western thinking and seem to be here to stay.

1900
Umberto I and Queen Margherita
Villa Lattanzi
Carrara

1962 Luciano Lattanzi
Semantic drawing
detail
Galerie Sydow
Frankfurt/Main

Words for art?

Are there any words for art? It has been said that if there were words which could describe a work of art or design completely, the work would be superfluous. This means that however well a work of art is being described or analysed, words cannot replace the direct visual experience. Naturally, there are words to describe art; anything can be discussed. It is important, perhaps, to remember that art is art and literature is literature, both disciplines in their own right. Words are largely used to convey information or in literature to compose as well a non-visual work of art. The question as to the possibility of describing art in words can only be answered reasonably well when we clearly distinguish between the character and function of the visual and non-visual arts. In any case the artist wants his work to communicate, to speak directly, to create a dialogue with the observer. To gain a true understanding of art, it is not only important to look at art, but to make art speak.

Dialogue and not monologue

A work of art is not a monologue but a dialogue, which is renewed by each generation and always in a different way. The work of art creates a dialogue in which the artist, the amateur, the collector, the visitor to museums and art galleries and those who are looking at reproductions or attending a lecture with projections of a work of art all take part. Each generation finds a new dialogue, each generation has its favoured masters and its favoured subjects, or in non-figurative art its favoured visual experiences. Each generation will reflect its own approach in the art of its period which achieves popularity and will tend to look at at least some of the works of the past generation in an unbelieving, doubting way.

We can look at one example of this in considering Kandinsky's thoughts on the subject. He certainly believed that a work of art should communicate and said so. 'A work of art consists of two elements, the inner and the outer. The inner is the emotion in the soul of the artist; this emotion has the capacity to evoke a similar emotion in the observer. The sequence is: emotion (in the artist), the senses, the work of art, the senses, emotion (in the observer). The emotions of the artist and of the observer will be alike and equivalent to the extent that the work of art is successful. In this respect painting is in no way different from a song: each is communication. The inner element, that is the emotion, must exist, otherwise the work of art is a sham. The inner element determines the form of the work of art.'

Vincent van Gogh
Breton women
detail
Galleria d'Arte Moderna
Milan

Wassily Kandinsky
(1866–1944)
Improvisation XIX
Städtische Galerie
Munich

Content

On occasions the observer will recognize immediately in a work of art or design the expression of basic, abstract feelings or of ideas in which he is really involved, and he will see the justification of such work without further explanations. On other occasions he will look in vain for an obvious content or merit but find, however, that such a work is nevertheless admired by a serious-minded art public who are simply attracted by the outstanding aesthetic qualities of the work, and who are not at all interested in any other justification. In fact does a work of art need such justification dictated by content? The observer will notice, perhaps with surprise, that a certain school of painting or sculpture or of the fine or applied graphic arts is held in great esteem because of the opinions expressed by leading creative artists, scholars and critics of art.

If justification by clarity and obviousness of content was the only *raison d'être* for art and design, very little experiment would be welcomed since experiments in all periods lead towards new ways of thinking and creating. Art would be very poor otherwise. From a superficial point of view, and especially in modern movements, art and design appear to be anything, composed in any way, done by anyone, but there is a more profound way of judging a work: the search for quality which might exist both in the art and anti-art of a certain period.

We have to keep in mind that content is not everything. Art, architecture and design are rather a combination of content and

Giacomo Manzù
(born 1908)
Cardinal
Galleria d'Arte Moderna
Milan

Wilhelm Busch
(1832–1908)
Heavily laden
Niedersächsische Landesgalerie
Hanover

physique. When content is not present or easy to find, we become more directly aware of it. Indeed, whereas the intellectual of the *avant-garde* might claim a complete lack of interest in content, the general public will perhaps, more often than not, strive to find at least some sort of explanation in a work of art or design. But this longing for explanation is not as important as it is sometimes supposed to be ; it is simply caused by the element of curiosity, the need for contrast, the desire for the non-available, which indeed are all part of the sub-conscious function of the human mind.

attributed to Matteo Civitali
(1436–1501)
Portrait of a youth
Victoria and Albert Museum
London

The subject matter

The subject matter is perhaps the principal aspect which the general public is attached to or attracted by when seeing art, and often it is the property of art that may motivate a person to study art, architecture, and design more closely. But the modern school does not make appreciation of a work of art or design depend on the subject matter. Non-figurative work often rejects the analysis of the subject matter and relies on the subconscious mind to react towards certain shapes and colours and compositions. Then how should one approach this topic? Perhaps it is true to say that the subject matter, in the fundamental sense of appreciation, has always been of secondary importance even though the artist, until he freed himself of patronage during the eighteenth century, was in many instances commissioned to produce a work of art according to the political, religious or social requirements of his patron. An aftermath of this development can be studied in most academy work of the turn of the century, when even though *avant-garde* work was well on its way, idealism and historical association were sold made to measure, in a period when frivolous nude studies could only pass when dressed-up as sentimentalities or symbols of virtue.

Acquiring a fair knowledge of political and religious and cultural events is the best aid to a full understanding and appreciation of the subject matter of art. Comparing and relating, seeking parallels in art and design with general tendencies, fashions and cultural interchanges, is a far more dignified and deserving approach towards the subject matter of a work of art or design than pure sentimentalism.

1969 Patrick Caulfield
Pottery
Tate Gallery
London

1971 Roberto Garcia York
Surrealistic composition
private collection

1958/63 Maria Vieira
*Moving circular surfaces
in spherical space*
aluminium
64 × 64 × 32·5 cm
Wilhelm Lehmbruck Museum
Duisburg

Representation, realism and abstraction

Pure representation is mainly a question of technique and skill, pure abstraction a product of the imagination ; a masterpiece of art or design is with some luck a combination of the two. In the nineteenth century most critics did not write about art as such but about representation and association. The artist of today still suffers from this aspect as the public is trained by tradition to see in art something which is representational, and it will generally not accept anything which does not conform with these principles.

A work of art may be created in such a way that a resemblance with a real object is visible, but it does not depend on this for being a work of art. Looking at the works of art created by humanity since the beginnings of art in pre-history it will be noticed that naturalistic representation and an exact optical realism is the exception rather than the rule. Perhaps only the works of classical Greek and Roman art, and of the Renaissance and art movements which followed them and were influenced by them, are an exception. Especially in academic art, which follows almost without exception the classic tradition, representation and realism never seem to cease and it was only in recent decades that the works of less orthodox artists were submitted to the most traditional national academies of the Western world.

An image is never absolute, it depends on the point of view, on the circumstances. Obviously, a frontal view differs from a view in profile. In some works of art the artist shows several view points at the same time because he does not want to be restricted to the limitations, the

1966 Alan Davie
Pan's castle no 1
oil on 2 canvases
84×96 in
Gimpel Fils Gallery
London

Alexander Calder
(born 1898)
Lithograph in colour
London Arts Gallery

monotony of only one view. This is to be found in Oriental, Egyptian,
and in Western medieval art which often show many scenes in one
painting. Picasso does the same. There are as many views about the
visual reality of an object as there are opinions in a lively discussion of a
particular subject. Whether one favours or not the message inherent in
the subject matter, the final judgement of a work will rely on the
aesthetic quality.

1969 *Objects*
weatherproof enamel on steel
exhibition Galerie Niepel
Düsseldorf :
Werner Nöfer
Ferdinand Kriwet
Otmar Alt
Peter Brüning
Gernot Bubenik

1965 Jack Youngerman
Springs
acrylic paint
83×72 in
Betty Parsons Gallery
New York

1949 Etienne Hajdu
Homage to Bela Bartok
copper
142·5×216 cm
Wilhelm Lehmbruck Museum
Duisburg

1970 Ceri Richards
Pastorale
from 'The Beethoven suite with
variations' screenprint
30 × 17¾ in (76·2 × 45 cm)
Marlborough Fine Art
London

1970 Ceri Richards
Major-minor orange blue
screenprint
29⅞ × 21¾ in (76 × 55 cm)
Marlborough Fine Art
London

Interpretation of a work of art

Works of art or design are not intrinsically more difficult to understand than works of music or of literature. Contrary to the belief of centuries, there is really nothing mysterious about the essence of art. Only the approach to an interpretation is different. Visual and non-visual artists are all equally important in establishing the spiritual and creative expression of an age or of a particular school or civilization.

The interpretation of a work of art is indeed similar to the interpretation of a work of music. For this reason the translation of a visual subject into physical terms, by painting or sculpting it, has been compared with the composition of a work of music. There are numerous examples of painters attempting to catch the impression of music on a canvas, and for centuries composers have been inspired by people and scenery, besides purely abstract feelings such as love and friendship, and have translated them into musical language.

In attending a concert, the public cannot easily escape from listening. In this sense a work of music is much more demanding than a work of art, which is usually exhibited together with many others. But even if a work of art were exhibited on its own, one could, by closing one's eyes, more easily escape the impact than one could prevent oneself from listening to music. In order to create equal conditions, one would have to show a work of visual art in complete isolation, perhaps to one visitor at a time and have just the right kind of information and background music available in order to create the right *ambiance*, allowing the fullest enjoyment and involvement possible.

Art, design and style

The porch of Freiburg Minster
photographed by the author

*c.*1550 Philibert de l'Orme
Château d'Anet
Courtauld Institute of Art
London

Although the Renaissance wa
introduced into France from
Italy *c.*1500, some French
architects clung to the
verticalism of the Gothic
period in certain
architectural details

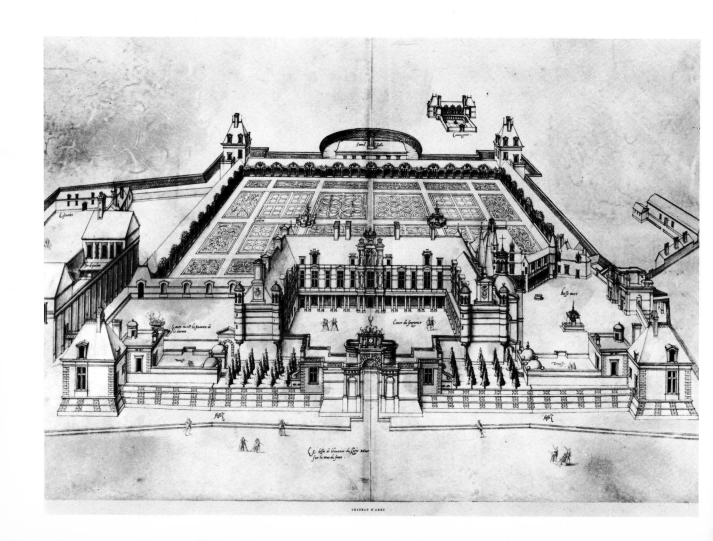

1446–51
Palazzo Rucellai Florence :
a hundred years before Anet
we find the Florentine
Renaissance inspired by the
style of ancient Rome

Can history help the designer?

The sequence of historical and creative experience is extremely important. The artist is born into a certain civilization and has to work for it and is influenced by it, and in this respect today's artist is in the same position as his predecessors. Materials have changed, of course. The development from writing to today's sophisticated techniques in graphic design and printing offer a good example. The invention of papyrus made possible the art of drawing, parchment gave rise to illumination ; the chisel was replaced by brush and quill. With the development of printing from movable types the scribe left the field to the compositor who today is facing a new situation : photosetting. With the invention of photography there was no longer any real need for 'reproduction' portraiture, although this is still being practised in our day. If the designer is a good artist he will not, however, content himself with existing materials and conventions. He will try to change things or at least explore the possibilities for change.

The teaching of art presents a problem. The colleges can provide facilities and lecturers, but cannot create artists. Klee observed : 'No good artist should teach and no one should teach who is not a good artist.' In training designers, creative talent must be blended with technology. Today, education can only guide the artist before he makes a living, in contrast to other times when the young artist lived in the house of his master and was dependent on him. Today, the young artist and designer studying at college is free in many ways but often has little moral support, as the lecturer has usually to divide his attention between too many students.

Freiburg Minster
an example of the Gothic skyline,
with Renaissance elements added
at a later date ;
photographed by the author

It is quite obvious that a real vocation is needed to teach design, at any level, in order to reach a high standard. The teaching of history, theory, and the aesthetics of art and design requires an ideal combination of knowledge and artistic imagination. In the teaching of design a knowledge of the technical aspects is complementary ; in the teaching of art and design appreciation the aesthetic and historical aspects complement each other. The teaching of design history is an important introduction to the student's own creative work. Design history will be of the greatest help if historic works are constantly compared with the student's own sphere of design. This is best achieved by teaching the entire subject, history of art and design, always on a comparative basis ; that is, comparison in terms of periods, of different branches of art, of national and international schools.

The history of art, in the sense of *analysing* and not merely *recording* periods and the life of artists, is a comparatively new subject, inspired by J. J. Winckelmann's *Geschichte des Altertums*, Dresden, 1764. Winckelmann has been called the spiritual father of art historians. A knowledge of art history may be acquired either by direct experience, with or without the guidance of a teacher, or indirectly through publications, although illustrations in books may be quite misleading, as they show the original work almost always on a reduced scale. They are certainly only an imperfect substitute for a direct experience of the work of art. In our age of television and easy facilities for travel, it is sometimes doubtful whether the copying of originals at museums

1647 Wenceslaus Hollar
Part of Westminster
with Parliament House,
Westminster Hall and the Abbey
British Museum
London:
the north is still a stronghold
of the Gothic style

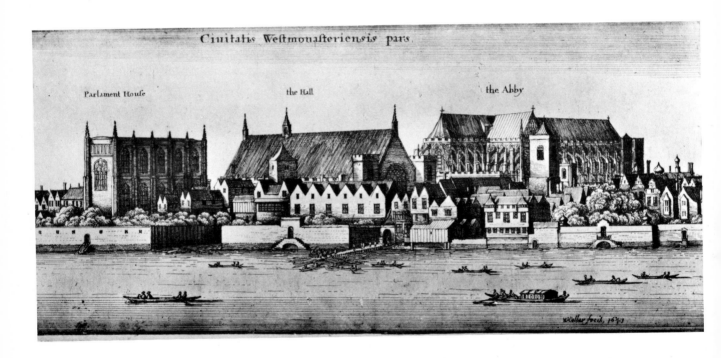

or from plaster casts is still justified, as an introduction to an analysis
of aesthetic aspects of art and of formal values such as proportions,
area, space, composition, line, light, and colour. A thorough
inspection of these is, no doubt, extremely useful to the future
designer and artist. Past styles should be, above all, judged critically
for quality. The right conception of basic elements of design should
be sought out, basic contrasts explored — light against dark, broad

1502 Donato Bramante
San Pietro in Montorio:
the south abandons the early
solid Renaissance feeling in
favour of a more swinging
Baroque style

against narrow, active against passive. By comparing Romanesque with Gothic, Renaissance with Mannerism, Baroque with neo-Classicism ; by finding out which was revival and which was new, from the Carolingian Renaissance to the art of our time ; by tracing the Classic and Romantic tendencies that have existed throughout the ages ; and by discovering the way in which function and beauty have been skilfully combined to create art, the student will perceive the changing nature of attitudes to aesthetic questions.

Art history is best taught in a rational and time-saving way by having the facts explained in lectures and seminars by lecturers with a wide cultural background in subjects other than their own and who have a knowledge of the intellectual, political and social conditions, which were usually responsible for the development of a particular style or school in a certain branch of art and design. In this way the young designer will learn from the past that he should design for today, or even for tomorrow, but not for yesterday. This is particularly important to the embryo designer because he will set out eventually to perform a service, and he will have to meet the many demands of modern society into which he is born : cultural, social, political, and industrial. Only if his work is good will it be judged by his own contemporaries and by future generations as art in its own right.

first half of 18th century
wrought iron
English
height 12 ft 1 in (368·3 cm)
Victoria and Albert Museum
London

Aesthetic vandalism or design?

The skilful collection and scrupulous selection of examples of art and design of the past and present can also help the designer to train his mind and sight. In any case, human nature has the desire to preserve the best of the past and to let the imagination travel into the past. This can only be recommended provided that in so doing the artist uses his aesthetic judgement positively. He will, however, find that relatively few witnesses are left to enable him to study fully the origins of art and design. Much was destroyed as was the case with furniture which was, to a certain extent, considered 'consumable material'. There is proof, for instance, that Queen Marie-Antoinette sent out specialists to find good parts in 'old-fashioned' furniture which was then dismantled in order to incorporate these good parts into new pieces of furniture. French kings are renowned for having sold their old furniture to make room for new and, even in those days, this was not considered anything unusual. In fact, it had been practised by the church for centuries by selling, for example, the altar-piece of a cathedral to make room for a new altar in the latest 'fashion'. In particular was this the case in the Baroque period when a great deal of valuable Gothic furniture was simply disposed of by being passed on to a small parish church which could not afford to commission a 'fashionable' artist. In the early nineteenth century, when neo-Gothic was the fashion of the day, the same damage was done by those who eagerly 'purified' the interior of churches by eliminating good Baroque furniture, with the best of intentions but through sheer ignorance. James Wyatt (1747–1813) earned himself the unflattering name of 'Wyatt the Destroyer' for his many ruthless

attributed to A. C. Boulle
(1642–1732)
furniture with Baroque and
Classical elements;
Wallace Collection
London

1766 Fournier le jeune
Manuel Typographique
Paris
Printers' ornaments and flowers
or fleurons, when proportionally
enlarged, frequently remind us of
contemporary ornament in
architecture and on furniture

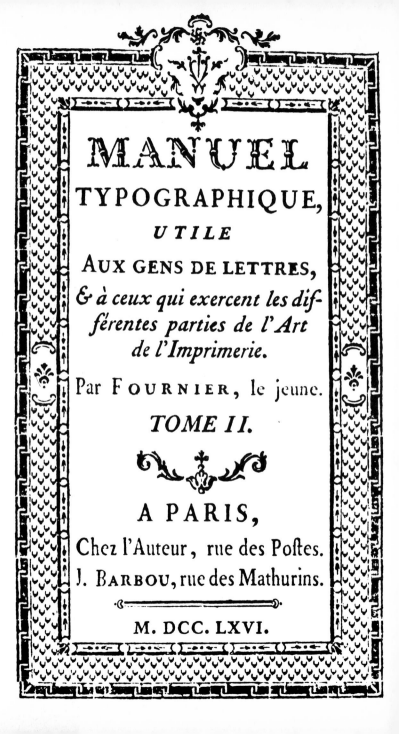

MANUEL
TYPOGRAPHIQUE,
UTILE
AUX GENS DE LETTRES,
*& à ceux qui exercent les dif-
férentes parties de l'Art
de l'Imprimerie.*

Par FOURNIER, le jeune.

TOME II.

A PARIS,
Chez l'Auteur, rue des Poftes.
J. BARBOU, rue des Mathurins.

M. DCC. LXVI.

1769
Augustinerkirche
Mainz

c.1790 Josiah Wedgwood
Portland vase
copy of the vase, made in unglazed
black stoneware at his factory at
Etruria, Staffordshire ;
The Jones Collection
Victoria and Albert Museum
London

restorations and 'betterments' to Gothic buildings, such as the cathedrals at Salisbury, Durham, and Hereford. This happened too in the case of town planning when, for example, a good deal of old Paris in the Latin Quarter was destroyed to make room for Viollet-le-Duc's ambitious plans, which is the more regrettable because the same artist did so much to restore and preserve scholarly Gothic art as in the cathedral of Notre Dame de Paris.

Compared with the history of mankind as a whole, the few decades available for collection and preservation represent only a short period. The right balance between preserving the best of the past and providing for the demands and needs of the future will guide the good designer in his decision. The designer is there to put things right.

1822–24 John Nash
All Souls
Langham Place
London:
Corinthian columns,
needle spire

Analysis of style

Much has been said about style in art and design but perhaps the most important fact to remember about styles is that names of styles cannot be used like 'labels'. Even today relatively little importance is given to the fact that styles, with the exception of those of the modern movement, were often called by their now established period names only generations after they had been developed and practised.

Gothic art, during its period, for instance, was called 'modern' or 'French' art. The expression Renaissance, related to the Renaissance of the arts on which Vasari reports in his *Le vite de' più eccellenti Architetti, Pittori et Scultori Italiani* of 1550, was to become an established period term in its own right only from about 1820 in France and from about 1860 in Germany with the publication of Jacob Burckhardt's *Die Kultur der Renaissance in Italien*. Mannerism, until very recently, did not rate as an independent art movement, but as a style attached to the High Renaissance. Only today do we consider Mannerism as a name for a style of painting, drawing, and sculpture, principally Italian, of the period from *c*.1520 until 1600 which cannot be classified as either Renaissance or Baroque. Baroque, like Gothic originally a derogatory term – from the Portuguese *barroco*=irregular shaped pearl, meaning also 'against all rules, curious in contrast, good taste' – needed centuries to gain full recognition. Rococo from the French *rocaille*=objects in the style of grottoes and mussels, even today is considered by many only as a more refined *finale* of Baroque. One could equally well ask the question: Where and when does neo-Classicism really begin?

There is enough proof that Palladio, the architect of the late Renaissance, was already copied by many architects as early as the seventeenth century. Other difficulties add to the confusion: the historicism and eclecticism of the nineteenth century which involved a revival and mixture of many styles from the past; the practice of authors, in writing about a certain period or style, of frequently borrowing generously not only from preceding and following periods, but even from loosely related styles.

However revealing it might be for the historian to acquire a knowledge of chronological dates, the immediate interest of the creative artist and designer lies more in seeing art periods in terms of styles. He will analyse a style as having particular characteristics and aesthetic requirements, as for instance the spatial arrangement in works of art and design during a certain period or within a certain school. The whole cultural reflection of a period in all fields of visual and non-visual art will perhaps interest him more than mere dates and anecdotes of the artists' lives of that time. This is a natural reaction, because the aesthetic experience of art of the past usually precedes theory about it. By this experience the artist becomes inspired to create new form, as the Impressionists were inspired by Japanese art or the Cubists by Negro sculpture. The influence and educational value of visits to exhibitions, with or without the direct intention to study, should not be underestimated.

Mosque Ketchaoua
Algiers:
a blend of oriental and European styles

Especially gratifying when analysing style and period, is the study of works of architecture. Perhaps more than in any other field of art and design, architecture reveals the *Formgeist* of a period. A study of architecture leads to the discovery of an ever-changing attitude towards form; the preference, expressed in different periods, may be in striking contrast, between a liking for the monumental, for the rustic and robust, for volume and masses, for height and verticalism, for horizontalism, for the gracefully elegant and ornamental, for the theatrical, for the *Sturm und Drang* of the start of a new era, or for historicism and revival, an over-cherishing of the past. Without calling the styles by their proper period term, the enlightened reader will be aware which particular style is referred to in the above list of characteristics. Architecture, often planned by one generation, is not necessarily built according to plan by the next, because this next generation has already acquired an entirely different set of formal attitudes. This is true in the case of the altered Gothic cathedrals or the palaces modernized during the Renaissance or the many secular buildings changed during the neo-Classical period.

Further, too little attention is paid to the many fields of applied design and the crafts which often yield more precise evidence of the spirit in forming a period than painting or sculpture. It should be borne in mind that painting is frequently influenced by the fashion of a certain school while the design of practical objects perhaps more directly expresses the needs and the spirit, the functional and artistic considerations of an epoch. We would indeed have a less complete

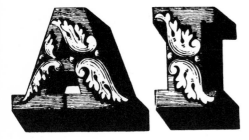

picture of the art of times past by an absence of Greek vases, Roman glass, Celtic jewellery and illuminated manuscripts, Gothic shrines, the writings and printed books of the Renaissance, the theatrical *décor* of Mannerism, the *trompe l'œil* ceilings of Baroque, and the magnificent interior decoration of Rococo and neo-Classicism. Equally valuable from this point of view are the so-called minor or applied arts of the past, and the great engineering achievements of the industrial age.

The letters of the alphabet, especially the inner shapes of such letters and of type, reveal not only the prevailing cultural fashion of the period, but often the different regional fashions. Architecture seems to have a corresponding parallel to letter forms. Often the inner shapes in works of architecture, in spite of being three-dimensional, remind us of the fashionable styles of writing and the typefaces of that time. Similar correspondences can be observed in the details and in the conception and distribution of walls, fenestration, the shapes of viaducts, the planning of courtyards, of squares and of streets and overall town planning. Printers' ornaments and flowers or *fleurons*, when proportionately enlarged, frequently remind us of the ornament used in architecture and on furniture of the same period. The fascinating ornaments of Fournier, the Paris printer, on the fringe between Baroque and Classicism, may serve as an example. Finally, even fashion, short-lived as it may be, can disclose not only personal taste but also reflect social changes and mirror the tendency towards revolution or the conservatism of an age.

Eduard Jakob von Steinle
(1810–86)
Portrait
Städelsches Kunstinstitut
Frankfurt/Main :
a Classical style in fashion

1890 Henri van de Velde
Abstract composition of plants
pastel
Rijksmuseum Kröller-Müller
Otterlo

Modern art and design

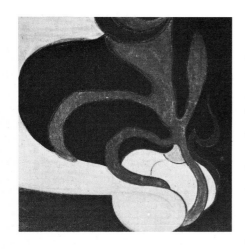

How far can a knowledge of art theory contribute towards a better understanding of contemporary art and design ? What indeed can be explained about modern art ? The conditions under which it was possible for a certain branch of art to flourish can be discovered. There are, however, a few crucial factors that cannot be calculated – the thoughts and talent of the artist who creates out of his spiritual attitude and his experience. The individual artist with an inner life of his own frequently interprets his experience in a quite different visual way to that of most of his fellow men. This difference has to no small extent multiplied the chaos experienced by a public confronted with non-figurative art. As an inspiration there is, no doubt, the rhythm of life itself, but how can it be translated into visual terms ? The artist who has the courage to depart from conventional ideas of life – what has he left to take as a source of ideas ? Only himself, his own philosophy.

The public will judge new things according to historical experience and established convention. It will often expect the new to be a repetition of the old and, therefore, will not understand that a new development in art has to be judged according to the new rules it creates. An experience with classical art – however valuable this may have been in educating the feeling for quality, style and greatness – does not necessarily help in understanding contemporary art. New art has to be experienced anew. However, if a new development of art demands to be judged by new rules, this does not necessarily mean that it condemns the past, that it regards masterpieces of the past as

Paul Cézanne
(1839–1906)
Les grandes baigneuses
National Gallery
London :
detail, centre panel
revealing the new pictorial
concept of Cézanne

wholly mediocre or as being of secondary importance. It is often the case that an artist of the modern movement can create anew out of his very knowledge of the past – although this inspiration is insuffient on its own. Experience of the past combined with experience of the present will enable the artist to find a language of his own more effectively. If a new art form fails, the artist cannot escape and go back to a former and safer style without losing his self-respect and faith. Picasso, on being asked whether he did not make a mistake in taking up his present style of art, admitted frankly that mistakes could not be avoided, but that it was at the same time quite impossible to

1908 Piet Mondrian
The red tree
70 × 99 cm
Gemeentemuseum
The Hague

1912/13 Piet Mondrian
Composition trees II
98×65 cm
Loan S. B. Slijper
Gemeentemuseum
The Hague

1917 Piet Mondrian
Composition no 3 with colour planes
48×61 cm
Gemeentemuseum
The Hague

1964 Josef Albers
Departing in yellow
30 × 30 in
Tate Gallery
London

1970 Erich Schulz-Anker
*Mathematical analysis
of letter forms*
D Stempel AG
Frankfurt/Main

return to the past and do his work in an earlier style which had long been surpassed by his actual visual attitude. From the observer's point of view, no problem is solved by those who, failing to understand the art of their time, return exclusively to classical art and also to applied design and architecture of the past. This would mean ignoring the present and living in the past. Only a positive approach towards art and design is truly constructive and can help find a new visual vocabulary which caters for the creative needs of today and tomorrow.

There is no general agreement about the application of the word modern art. Used in the sense of our time, some experts believe a work of art in a museum of modern art should not be more than fifty years old. Others who are more concerned with historical accuracy, and want to show the roots of modern development, assert that Cézanne and the artists of French Impressionism are the spiritual fathers of modern art and want to keep them in. Indeed, entirely new pictorial structures were achieved by Cézanne and the Impressionists at a time when in most European countries the art of painting had frequently declined to almost photog aphic reproduction.

Carel Visser
Eight beams
iron, wood
length 300 cm
Rijksmuseum Kröller-Müller
Otterlo

Mathematics and modern art

Do modern art and design depend too much on a mathematical approach ? It has often been said that some artists of our time are reducing art simply to mathematical terms and, therefore, the 'soul of creation' is being lost completely. Leonardo was convinced that only out of a combination of both temperament and mathematics could true art be created. Ignoring purely creative considerations, any style and period of art of the past or of today shows certain calculations made by the artist, subconsciously or consciously, which result in a kind of geometrical grouping in the intended composition. These calculations are often directly or indirectly related to the proportions of the human body as has already been demonstrated.

Such mathematical considerations together with a personal, individual feeling for proportions are the indispensable tools of any creative process. In this connexion it would be revealing to compare the rather mathematical grouping of people shown in pictures, who were often scaled up or down in size according to their relative importance and distance. This held from the time of ancient Egypt to the Renaissance when the principles of perspective came to provide for a proportional grouping and to solve the question of visual priority by basically mathematical rules. It is natural that artists around the turn of the century should break away from these principles and try to prove that art is possible without obeying slavishly the principles of perspective. In fact they often reject perspective because they feel the artist should not be forced into the straitjacket of rules while searching for instinctive solutions of composition, interpretation of size, importance,

1967 André Volten
Steel construction
Rijksmuseum Kröller-Müller
Otterlo

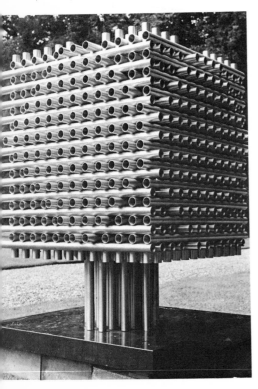

depth, and distance. A rejection of such individualism of approach seems justified only if the artist in question has completely disregarded the basic principles of good form.

Certainly mathematical thinking was advocated by the *avant-garde* Constructivists, and Mondrian probably more than any other artist departed in the early years of the century from that which people so far had considered art, thus creating compositions with entirely abstract means. Perhaps his pictures were supposed not to be an end in themselves but rather to mark a departure from conventional thinking. From this departure a new spirit was to be infused into art, and even today we draw inspiration from it. Contrary to common belief, in experiments of this kind art does not lose its 'soul' or its humanistic aspect. In fact, in modern art and design, proportions and attitudes can often be traced that reflect timeless principles. The early experiments of a restrained character were to become the 'architecture' on the basis of which a new concept could flourish. Furthermore, they have inspired recent attempts to re-design functional objects. After many decades we probably realize only today the great influence upon contemporary applied design of this pioneer work in fine art. Often these pioneer attempts had to wait many years before being applied and even longer before being appreciated by the general public. It is well to keep in mind that mathematics alone do not create design. Talent, instinct, and intellect are needed to achieve a satisfactory and aesthetically acceptable result.

1971 Iginio Balderi
Hard and soft forms
polyester
length 250 cm
private collection

1925 Le Corbusier
Violin, glass and bottles
31¾ × 45¾ in
Galerie Beyeler
Basle

Figurative art today?

Is figurative art still possible? The Renaissance tried to develop the classical aspect of art and to transform it and to adapt it to the needs of the approaching age of reason — thus serving as a bridge between the classical and the modern way of thinking. It is, therefore, ideally suited to close the gap between classical and modern art appreciation. The gulf between opposing opinions lies in the acceptance or non-acceptance of non-figurative art. Figurative art reappears time after time in the development of modern art and design. During the late 1910s and early 1920s, when the movement towards abstraction was still in full swing, but hardly taken up universally, Picasso, for instance, was already turning his back on Cubism which, with Braque, he had invented only a few years before. He was now painting his so-called monsters, big, colossal women who were, no doubt, inspired by the super-sculpture of official classical art of late Roman antiquity. In fact, by about 1925 he was fully neo-realistic. Into this period falls the propagation of new objective painting, *Die neue Sachlichkeit*, which was to have a great impact upon parallel developments in art and design movements such as the Purism of Ozenfant and Le Corbusier. These, in turn, were to inspire more especially the publicity art of the mid 1920s with its neo-realistic and symbolic posters which are so typical of that period.

1955 Reg Butler
Torso Summer
bronze
95·5×42×34·2 cm
Wilhelm Lehmbruck Museum
Duisburg

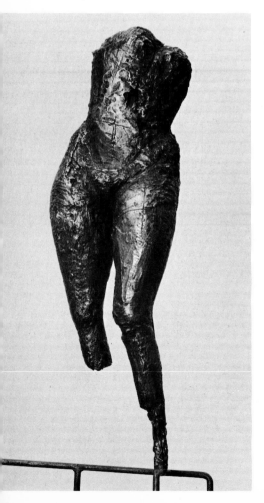

In this connexion it is as well to distinguish between the new realism of which, for instance, social realism is a branch, and the mere realistic approach of official painters, be it court painters of the past or artists serving modern propaganda. The latter appeal, above all, to people's sentiments and may be more concerned with suitably tailored and persuasive propaganda than with true aesthetic values.

It is quite natural that some of the painters teaching at the Bauhaus in the 1920s, Schlemmer and Feininger, for example, were also neo-realist and symbolic, yet worked alongside their more abstract colleagues such as Kandinsky and Klee.

In more recent years Pop art has reintroduced a tendency towards an obvious degree of realism and there are many other schools which never completely broke away from such realism, although seeking a new pictorial language. The tremendous impact of the new figurative Pop art image is indisputable. There certainly is a natural desire in many human activities for both abstraction and realism to symbolize as well as to record. Even in the age of photography, film, and television the camera has not entirely replaced the desire for a more flexible visual realism.

1956 Lynn Chadwick
Stranger II
iron, plaster, cement
109 × 87 × 30 cm
front view
Wilhelm Lehmbruck Museum
Duisburg

1956 Lynn Chadwick
Stranger II
iron, plaster, cement
109 × 87 × 30 cm
back view
Wilhelm Lehmbruck Museum
Duisburg

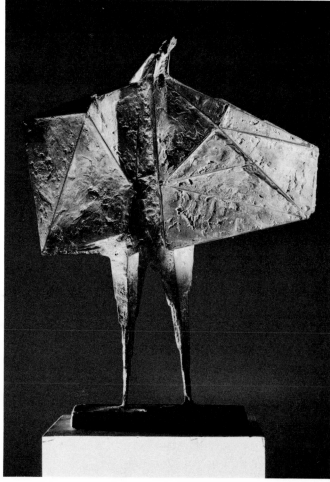

1965 George Segal
Girl in doorway
plaster, wood, glass, aluminium paint
113 × 63½ × 18 in
Whitney Museum of American Art
New York

Tomorrow

It is quite obvious that a judgement of a work of art or of a design product can never be final and criticism never inviolable. Even the most perceptive of critics and connoisseurs has his limitations and may find himself at a loss for words where the deepest feelings of an artist are expressed. Only the observer who tries to reconstruct in his mind the impressions of the artist will be able to understand truly an individual work of art. It certainly does not help towards a better understanding to generalize about art any more than it does to generalize about our fellow men or the customs and habits of other countries. In fact, it is impossible to answer questions on art in general terms. Discussion will only be fruitful if the people taking part have a precise knowledge of the subject. While taste is debatable, quality is unquestionable and therefore we would do well to try to develop an appreciation of quality.

It is also as well to keep in mind that in all periods there are artists of only limited achievement working alongside the few geniuses. Only those who become famous are finally remembered. Should only a few artists of today's young *avant-garde* generation ever achieve a world-wide reputation, their attempt to create new art forms will not have been in vain. We, their contemporaries, have the opportunity to help in arriving at a fair assessment of the modern masters. Therefore we should study the contemporary work of art critically and always consider whether it fulfils the first condition of art : beauty. If it does not, it may be not art at all. We should be conscious of this task and remember that perhaps upon our opinion depends which young artists of today will be the old masters of tomorrow.

Acknowledgments

The author had the good fortune of working, not for the first time, with Herbert Spencer and John Taylor of Lund Humphries. He wishes to thank them sincerely for their pleasant, encouraging and enthusiastic co-operation at all stages in the production of the book. Gratefully the author acknowledges the generous help of his colleague G. V. Davies in reading and discussing the text of this book, a task which he loyally carried out until its completion.

Although this thesis was written very recently, it is inspired by years of lecturing by the author in higher education in London and as a guest speaker at conferences in Britain and abroad. It also has its origins in the writing of hundreds of special features for international publications on a wide range of subjects on art and design as well as in broadcasting and the arrangement of educational exhibitions. Above all, it is the direct result of thousands of miles of travelling to meet artists and designers to obtain direct information and some original and hitherto unpublished illustrations. Many photographs were specially taken by the author. Although great care has been exercised in providing a reliable guide to historical developments, in many instances, in order to introduce the work of some younger artists and designers, illustrations of newer works are shown rather than works which can be easily consulted in collections and in art publications which are generally available. By this means, the author hopes also to give a lively picture of most of the more recent developments in art and design. In the course of compiling this thesis, several hundred original documents and publications in English, French, German and Italian were consulted, but simply for technical data, while the author has attempted to keep his own observations as personal and uninfluenced as possible. A few theoretical sources are offered for comparison, especially to illustrate the different approaches to aesthetic criticism over the centuries and to show the thinking of the *avant-garde* that was to influence profoundly today's art and our outlook on visual matters.

The author hopes the reader will wish to consult current publications for information to complement the ideas and material given in this book. The author suggests the term *visual aesthetics* because he envisages this field of study as an integral discipline, indispensable to the wide and varied domains of human expression.

1970 Henry Moore
Composition
marble
Forte dei Marmi studio
Foto Cav. I. Bessi
Carrara

The author wishes to express his gratitude to the following and to those mentioned in the captions of the book for information, documents, photographs, inspiration and suggestions. Page references indicate photographic acknowledgements.

Algerian Ministry of Information 217
Austrian Embassy 12
Bertoni 36
Cav. I. Bessi 173 179 235 238
Max Bill
British Museum, London
Bundesbildstelle Bonn 109 138
Rudolph Burckhardt 198
Professor Dr Carlos Cid Priego
Geoffrey Clements 232
Professor Sir William Coldstream
Courtauld Institute of Art, London
Harry Croner 141b
Crown copyright 211
Design Council, London
Deutsche Zentrale für Fremdenverkehr 111a 136 152 213
Dienst aus Deutschland 101c 124a 145b 147a
U. Edelmann 64
ENIT 205 209

Germano Facetti
Ferruzzi 92
Colin Forbes
Foto-Kessler 157a
French Government Tourist Office 35
Gimpel Fils Gallery, London
Dagmar Grauel-Korn 51b 194 199 230 231
Professor Dr Walter Gropius
Arno Hammacher 150 227
Robert Häusser 20a
Hawkley Studio 157b
Yves Hervochon 193b
IN-Bild 86 100b 111b 141a 144
Italian Institute
Hans Kuh, Novum Gebrauchsgraphik
Karel Kuklik 100
La Rinascente, Milan
Corrado, Luciano and Danilo Lattanzi
Dr Brigitte Lohmeyer, German Embassy
London Arts Gallery
Dr Peter Ludwig
Marlborough Fine Art, London
Moisio 106
Bernhard Moosbrugger 105a
Bruno Munari
Gabriele Muschel 171
National Gallery, London
Professor Alexander Nesbitt
Österreichische Lichtbildstelle 12 140

Photo Studios Ltd 116
Pablo Picasso
Publifoto 107
Rank Xerox, Milan
Rheinische Bildstelle 161
Royal Academy of Arts, London
Royal Norwegian Embassy
Jan Ságl 101
Erich Schulz-Anker, D. Stempel AG
F. lli Scrocchio 55
Albert Singer
Georges Souriau, Unesco Paris
Spanish Ministry of Information 30
Stadtverkehrsbüro Salzburg 38
Walter Steinkopf 78 79 80 120
Stickelmann 39a
Bert Stolk 63
Herbert Sulzbach, German Embassy
Otto Swoboda 38
Tate Gallery, London
Frank J. Thomas 13
Thorbjørn Tufte 34
Turkish Embassy 160
Victoria and Albert Museum, London
Karl Vöhringer, Form und Technik
Votava 76
Wallace Collection, London
Dr Weinsziehr

Further reading

Braque, Georges : *Cahiers 1917–1947*. Paris and New York 1948.

Croce, Benedetto : *Aesthetic* 1909. Vision Press and Peter Owen, London 1962.

Doesburg, Theo van : *Principles of neo-plastic art*. 1925. Lund Humphries, London 1969.

Ehrenzweig, Anton : *The hidden order of art*. Weidenfeld and Nicholson, London 1967.

Fry, Roger : *Vision and design*. 1920. Penguin Books, Harmondsworth 1961.

Gabo, Naum : *Of divers arts*. Faber & Faber, London 1957.

Hogarth, William : *Analysis of beauty*. 1753. Oxford University Press 1955.

Itten, Johannes : *The art of color*. Reinhold, New York 1961.

Kandinsky, Wassily : *Concerning the spiritual in art*. 1912. George Wittenborn, New York 1947.

Klee, Paul : *Notebooks Vol. 1: The thinking eye.* 1956. Lund Humphries, London 1961.

Le Corbusier : *The modulor.* 1948. Faber & Faber, London 1954.

Leijohnhielm, Christer : *Colours, forms and art*. Almqvist & Wicksell, Stockholm 1967.

Malevich, Kasimir : *The non-objective world.* 1927. Paul Theobald, Chicago 1959.

Moholy-Nagy, László : *The new vision*. 1928. George Wittenborn, New York 1947.

Mondrian, Piet : *Plastic art and pure plastic art*. George Wittenborn, New York 1951.

Munari, Bruno : *Discovery of the circle*. Alec Tiranti, London 1966.

Newton, Eric*: The meaning of beauty*. 1959. Penguin Books, Harmondsworth 1967.

Ostwald, Wilhelm : *Colour science*. Windsor & Newton, Harrow 1931.

Ozenfant, Amédée : *Foundations of modern art*. 1931. Dover Publications, New York 1952.

Pevsner, Nikolaus : *An outline of European architecture*. 1943. Penguin Books, Harmondsworth 1970.

Reynolds, Joshua : *Discourses on art*. Oxford University Press 1960.

Ruskin, John : *The lamp of beauty*. 1843–1883. Edited by Joan Evans. Phaidon, London 1959.

Scott, Geoffrey : *The architecture of humanism*. 1914. Methuen, London 1961.

Spencer, Herbert : *Pioneers of modern typography*. Lund Humphries, London 1969.

Vasari, Giorgio : *Lives of the artists*. 1550. Penguin Books, Harmondsworth 1970.

Venturi, Lionello : *History of art criticism*. E. P. Dutton, New York 1964.

Winckelmann, J. J. ; *History of ancient art*. Dresden 1764.

Wölfflin, Heinrich : *The sense of form in art*. Chelsea Publishing, New York 1958.

Index